PUBLISHING SECRETS EVERY AUTHOR SHOULD KNOW (BUT MOST DON'T)

Stephanie J Hale

www.oxfordwriters.com

COPYRIGHT

Copyright 2016 Stephanie J. Hale
www.stephaniejhale.com

ISBN: 978-0-9928460-7-7
The moral right of the author has been asserted.

All rights reserved. Apart from any fair dealing for the purposes of research or private study, or criticism or review, as permitted under the Copyright, Designs and Patents Act 1988, this publication may only be reproduced, stored or transmitted, in any form or by any means, with the prior permission in writing of the copyright owner, or in the case of the reprographic reproduction in accordance with the terms of licences issued by the Copyright Licensing Agency. Enquiries concerning reproduction outside those terms should be sent to the publisher.

Powerhouse Publications
94/124 London Road,
Oxford
OX3 9FN

Print Edition

British Library Cataloguing in Publication Data.
A catalogue record for this book is available from the British Library.

Contents

So You Want Write a Book? 7

How to Increase the Chances of Your Non-Fiction Book Selling 10

Should I Disguise Real-Life People in My Book or Will I Be Sued? 13

Can I Trust a Publisher Not to Steal My Book Idea? 15

How to Stop Other Writers Stealing Your Book or Film Idea 18

Should I Use *50 Shades of X* as a Book Title? 20

Can I Quote From Books, Songs or Poems Without Permission? 22

3 Tips to Avoid Distractions While You're Writing 26

How To Write Your Book Faster 28

How To Choose A Bestselling Book Title 30

How To Find A Publisher Or Literary Agent For Your Book 35

My Literary Agent Can't Sell My Book – What Should I Do? 38

"All Publishers Are Idiots!" 40

What About Writer's Block? 41

Should I Self-Publish My Non-Fiction Book or is a Mainstream Publisher Better? 42

The Difference Between Vanity Publishing and Self-Publishing 44

Why Some Authors Are "Luckier" Than Others! 46

How to Choose the Right Literary Agent For Your Book 51

How to Annoy Literary Agents 54

Red Flags to Watch Out for in Your Publishing Contract – What Authors Unwittingly Sign Away 56

What Do Publishers' Rejection Letters *Really* Mean? 60

Your Book Can Be a Massive Bestseller – Even If Publishers Have Rejected It! 62

Will Publishers Accept or Reject Your Book? 64

An Agent Or Publisher Has Rejected Your Book – Why it Pays to Keep Going 68

Publication Day – The Most Disappointing Day Of Your Life? 70

How to Write a Marketing Plan or Your Book 72

How to Choose The Best Book Cover 75

Which Sells Best: E-Books or Paperbacks? 79

How to Get a Celebrity Endorsement For Your Book 84

Should You Print More Copies of Your Self-Published Book or Is This Madness? 88

Why It Pays to Grow a List of Fans on Social Media 91

How To Turn Your Book into an Amazon Best Seller 93

How To Get Your Book Serialized in Newspapers and Glossy Magazines 95

Why Bother with Journalists? It Sounds Like Too Much Effort! 99

How to Prepare for a Radio or Television Interview 101

How To Fill A Room And Market Your Event in 7 Easy Steps 104

Would You Let TV Cameras into Your Home? 108

Do You Have What It Takes to Be a Millionaire Author? 111

How to Make More Money from Your Book 114

How to Host a Book Launch that Doesn't Suck 116

How Much Should Authors be Paid to Speak at Events? 122

What I Learned From Selling Books From the Back of My Car 127

The Author 131

The Authors' Vault FREE Training and Bonuses Specially for You 132

Oxford Literary Consultancy Publishing Services 133

For my wonderful children, Cormac, Tierni and Chiara

So You Want Write a Book?

So you want to write a book, but perhaps you're daunted by the odds? Believe it or not, there is a way to stack the cards in your favour – though less than 5 per cent of writers seem to know it.

Most new authors are so fired up with their ideas that they launch straight into writing their book without thinking about how they're going to sell it. But if you want to give yourself a head-start, then it's worth spending the time doing some research before you write a word.

How Publishers Think

When a literary agent or publisher looks at a book, they want to know it will sell. It is as simple as that. They want to know your book will make money. I will be blunt: if you are a good writer, if your writing is polished, if you are entertaining and witty, that is the icing on the cake. What matters most is whether there is an established market for your book, whether it's likely to sell and what quantities.

Consider this: 70 per cent of books published don't make a profit or even earn back their advance. This is why you need to do as much research as you can, before you make a start on Chapter 1.

The approach 95 per cent of writers take is to write a book and then think: "who will I sell it to?" In fact, a slight shift of thinking is needed. First of all, you need to identify your target readership. Suppose you are a divorce lawyer writing a book. Are you writing for the general public, law students, professional barristers or judges, for example? Each of these will have different questions and challenges. They'll all read a book for different reasons.

Importantly, once you have identified your specific target audience, you can then understand what motivates them. It also enables a publisher, ultimately, to market your book as they can work out where your readers "hang out" online and offline – magazines, clubs, associations, e-zines, etc. – so that they can target their publicity.

Profile Your Readers

Ideally, once you have identified your target audience, you need to step inside their shoes so that you can write a "profile" for them:

- Are they male or female?
- What kind of vocabulary do they use?
- How old are they?
- What are their top three goals?
- What do they like reading?
- Which clubs and associations do they belong to?
- Which publications do they read or subscribe to?
- What are their top three frustrations?
- What makes them angry?
- What makes them happy?

When you understand your readers, you start to understand

the triggers that make them search out your book, their emotional buttons, and the buzzwords they are likely to use. You can then provide some of the solutions to their problems if you're writing a non-fiction book. Or, if you're writing a novel, you can ensure you understand the conventions of a specific genre and add your own unique twist.

In essence, you are working out what your readers are looking for in their dream book before you start writing it.

How to Increase the Chances of Your Non-Fiction Book Selling

Want to increase your chances of writing a bestselling book right from the get-go? Here are some tips used by the top 5 per cent of authors.

Many successful writers do considerable research before they even get started writing their books. Much of this relies on having a basic understanding of marketing.

What Sells Books?

Let's go back to the fundamentals of what sells. Why do people buy books? Usually, it's the "what's in it for me" – or WIFM – factor. They buy because:

- they can learn something;
- it improves their life in some way;
- it saves them money;
- it solves a problem;
- they've loved other similar books.

To put it another way, people buy for "pain or gain". In other words, there is a pain in their life that needs solving. Or they think they will gain in some way – either emotionally or financially, or simply because they're already a big fan of a particular genre.

It is worth noting that one of the most powerful motivations in marketing is financial gain. In other words, a reader can justify "investing" in a book if they think it will either save them time or money. The trick is to think how you can apply these principles to your own book. This is particularly helpful for non-fiction, though perhaps less so for novels or poetry.

Your Book Title

A book title is one of the most powerful tools for selling a book. It gives the reader a succinct and clear reason for buying your book. Your title can make all the difference between a best-selling book and a book that ends up on the pile of rejected manuscripts. The important thing to remember is to put the benefit (WIFM) for the reader in the title.

Examples might be:

- A book targeted at would-be lawyers – *UK Law Made Easy* or *Everything You Need to Know About Crown Court* (WIFM: training).

- A book targeted at the general public – *Top Tips To Cut Your Lawyer's Fees in Half* or *How To Write Your Own Will* (WIFM: saving money).

- A book targeted at a specific niche – *The Landlord's Guide to Evicting Problem Tenants* or *How to Claim Compensation After an Accident at Work* (WIFM: problem solving).

- A book targeted at other lawyers – *What You Don't Know About Rival Law Firms* or *How To Become A Partner In Your Law Firm In Less Than A Year* (WIFM: competitive edge).

- A humorous book illustrated with cartoons – *100 Bizarre Court Cases* or *20 Most Stupid Judges* (WIFM: entertainment)

These titles are off the cuff and imperfect. But hopefully you can see the "what's in it for me" principle at work and see why a target audience would want to buy them.

This doesn't mean that a book has to be solely about the subject matter in the title. This just provides a convenient marketing "angle" for a book so that readers (and publishers, in the first instance) can see the benefits and understand why people would buy it.

Looking at the aforementioned titles, I hope that you can see that some books provide a more powerful motivation for buying than others. Saving money, making money, and problem-solving are stronger emotional motivations than entertainment or curiosity, for example.

Market Research

Thanks to the Internet, you can now do comprehensive research into what your readers are likely to be looking for. You can check amazon.com to see if there are any comparable books on the subject. This will help you to identify your unique selling points. Why, for example, would a reader choose to buy your book over others? What do you offer that other authors don't?

Don't be put off if there are similar books to yours. This shows that there is a market for your subject matter. However, you do need to identify what is special and different about your book to make it stand out.

Should I Disguise Real-Life People in My Book or Will I Be Sued?

Writers often ask me if it's OK to write about people they know. Sometimes they're writing a memoir or autobiography. Or perhaps they're writing a novel with a hero or villain based on someone they know.

There are various little tricks you can use to make sure that people don't recognize themselves. You can change physical appearance – stature, hair length, eye colour, etc. You can also change gender, profession, or location. Or you can blend two or more different people together to create a different character.

Believe it or not, there is a very good chance that most people *won't* recognize themselves. I say this as someone who has both written about other people and been written about as a character.

When I have created characters based on people I know, they have never spotted themselves! Never. Not once. Similarly, I failed to recognize a thinly-disguised portrait of myself in a Booker-shortlisted novel. Thankfully, the portrait was a flattering one. Though I won't tell you the name of the book – that's a little secret between me and the author!

Another alternative is to use a *nom de plume* to obscure everyone's identity, including your own. The creative advantage is that this may allow you the emotional freedom to write your book in an uninhibited way. Belle de Jour is a high-profile example of a writer who did this. In fact, this is quite common among writers of erotica, for obvious reasons. However, I wouldn't recommend this unless there is a good reason – as it makes it extremely difficult to do marketing and publicity once the book is published.

How will you promote your book if you can't speak to the media, for example? How will you manage your website or have an author page on Amazon? How will you build a relationship with your readers? People also relate better to book reviews when they see a photo of the author.

If you're on good terms with the people you're writing about, and you don't intend to disguise them, I'd advise asking what their feelings are. As a child, my mother was a newspaper journalist who used to pen witty columns about our home life. It was trivial domestic stuff, nothing to shake the earth. But as a teenager, it was excruciating. (And no, thankfully, you won't find any copies online. There was no internet back in those days!)

Much will come down to the personalities of the people you are writing about and what your relationship with them is like. Some people are flattered to be written about. Others may feel exposed, vulnerable or even offended. Only you will know the answer to this.

Finally, we come to the issue of libel. Now, libel laws are complex – I could easily write a whole book on the subject. However, the main question to ask is: can the person be identified by themselves or anyone else? If so, is what you've written damaging to them either professionally or personally?

Rest assured that libel is extremely hard to prove, very expensive, and rarely embarked upon by anyone but the rich and famous. This said, get expert advice if you think you may be writing anything that's likely to end up with a lawsuit.

Can I Trust a Publisher Not to Steal My Book Idea?

A new author came to me recently saying he'd been advised not to pitch his brilliant book idea to Hay House Publishing "in case they *steal* the idea."

Well that certainly made me choke and splutter on my fruit smoothie first thing in the morning. The thought of publishing icon, Louise Hay, stealing someone else's idea. Crikey, did I hear that correctly? I asked the author to repeat what he'd just told me. And yes, he was certain this was the advice that he'd been given.

I'd like to dispel a big myth here about publishers nicking book ideas off unsuspecting, naïve authors.

Publishers are inundated with book ideas. Some of them are receiving over 1,000 manuscripts per *day*. Do they really need to pinch your book idea when they can barely cope with what they're being sent already?

Just supposing that an editor did this in a moment of madness, would they get away with it? In this Internet age, when blogging and social media are prevalent, how on earth would they keep this secret? Wouldn't we all know about it via viral media? They might get away with it once. But twice? A dozen times? A hundred times? How would the publishing house stay in business when authors stopped sending them their manuscripts?

I've been working in the media and publishing for over 20 years now. I've yet to witness anything that convinces me that this actually happens. What I do see though – and regularly – is opportunists taking advantage of authors' anxiety that this might happen. Because guess what? It just so happens that the "experts" who share such nuggets of wisdom usually have a service that will protect your intellectual property at a price. Or they'll even offer to publish it for you too. Gee, thanks!

Cowboy publishing experts aside, if you're really worried about your idea being copied, you can ask the other party to sign a "non-disclosure agreement" (NDA) or simply trademark your book title. Be warned though that NDAs are off-putting to most publishers and literary agents unless, for example, you have good reason to hide your identity.

It is also difficult to completely trademark a title, as it's still relatively easy to mimic a brand. Take, for example, my event, The Millionaire Bootcamp for Authors, which was later "copied" under the title of The Millionaire Summit for Authors by one of my attendees. You only need to change one word in order to mimic a successful title and there are so many variations.

There's an understandable anxiety in many authors that your great idea might be used by someone else. You may worry that another writer will have the same book title as you, will launch a book with a similar plot or topic, or that they'll write in a similar style. When you find a book with the same idea, you may worry that "someone else got there first" or "there's no point me writing my book now".

But here's the good news. At time of writing this, there are 7.5 billion people on this planet: more than enough to go around for everyone. No one else is ever going to write with your unique voice, your passion, your dedication, your amazing experience. Another book may have the same title or plot. But it's impossible to replicate *you*.

You don't need to reinvent the wheel – and sometimes it's a great advantage to "piggyback" off someone else's fantastic idea. One only has to think of Helen Fielding's novel *Bridget Jones' Diary* (1996) which breathed fresh life into Jane Austen's classic, *Pride and Prejudice*.

Some literature experts argue that there's only a limited number of archetypal plots in all books, whether fiction or non-fiction. The generally accepted point of view is that there is only *one* basic plot, i.e. there is a problem – the problem is explored – the problem is resolved. In novels, this problem is usually dealt with in a sequence that typically follows the pattern of: exposition – rising action – climax – falling action – denouement. This pattern can be repeated once or many times throughout a book. In non-fiction, the template is often, broadly speaking, that of: here's the problem, now here's the solution. Rinse and repeat.

With over two million books already published worldwide each year, it's unlikely anyone will come up with a totally fresh and original idea. But your wisdom, your enthusiasm, your vision will always be as unique as your fingerprint. And no one can ever steal that from you.

How to Stop Other Writers Stealing Your Book or Film Idea

Authors and scriptwriters are often worried that someone might steal their book or film idea. They become nervous once they start sending out their manuscript to agents or producers.

If this is a topic that's worrying you, here are some of the main points to consider:

1. **Date-stamped mail:** A simple way to safeguard your copyright used to be to send a copy of your manuscript to yourself via registered mail, ensuring that the package was date-stamped. You could then leave the envelope sealed. While this is no longer valid in a court of law, it may be sufficient as a psychological deterrent.

2. **Register your work:** There are a number of companies that offer to "hold" your manuscript for you or register it for a small fee. In my opinion, this is unnecessary. However, if it sets your mind at rest, this is an option to consider.

3. **Ideas and concepts:** Be aware that there is no copyright for an "idea" or a "concept". This is because there are very few original book or film ideas. Most ideas are workings or reworkings of archetypal or classic plot lines.

4. **What is unique?** What makes a plot unique is the writer who writes it. I've used the following example many times to illustrate this point: consider *Romeo and Juliet* and then *West Side Story*. Same plot, different writer. You could say that Stephen Sondheim stole the idea from Shakespeare.

Yet the new story set in 1950s New York is a masterpiece in its own right.

5. **Professional reputation**: Agents and producers work hard to build up their reputation for excellence and professionalism. They wouldn't last 5 minutes if they started stealing clients' ideas. In this Internet age, where millions of people are connected via blogs, e-zines and social media, word would soon get about. You can quickly and easily check out the credentials of most book and film professionals simply by using Google.

6. **Your passion:** Every writer has their own passion. I might love the pitch for a thriller set on a desert island or in outer space. But the fact is, I could never write it even if I researched it. Passion is the hidden ingredient that gives writing its energy, vibrancy and appeal. No one else will ever be able to write like you.

Should I Use *50 Shades of X* as a Book Title?

Here's a question I am frequently asked:

"If I decided to write a book inspired by *50 Shades of Grey,* and called it *50 Shades of X* – the only similarity being a similar-sounding title – is that possible without a big lawsuit, or would it be better to write *69 Shades of Y?*"

The answer to this applies to all "spin-off" titles that allude to a *hot* book or movie that's on everyone's lips.

First of all, check if the phrase is trademarked. If it is, then the answer is clearly: "No, you can't."

If it isn't then, yes, you can go ahead.

Perhaps more important though is the next step. Check to see how many other people have also thought of your idea.

A quick bit of market research reveals:

- 50 Shades of Nylon
- 50 Shades of DASH Diet
- 50 Shades of Green
- 50 Shades of Gravy
- 50 Shades of Classical
- 50 Shades of Red Riding Hood
- And so on …

These titles cover everything from books to DVDs to MP3s. The topics range from Irish songs, to dieting, to social media marketing, to cookery. So there is very little scope here to establish your own special brand or unique selling point.

This isn't to say that you shouldn't piggyback off another writer's great idea – especially if you can put your own unique spin on the subject. For example, there have been at least 17 different movie adaptations of *Alice in Wonderland* since its first publication in 1865. These have included: *Betty Boop in Blunderland* (1934); the well-known children's Disney animation (1951); an X-rated musical comedy focusing on the weird sexual undertones (1976); a *Care Bears Adventure in Wonderland* (1987); and Tim Burton's darkly surreal movie starring Johnny Depp.

You might wonder why there have been so many adaptations. But "re-purposing" or imitation of an already successful brand is in many ways an incredibly smart move. Someone else has already tested the market before you and proved a formula to be successful. There is a clear readership and target market – a publisher's dream. Everyone knows *the brand*. So in many ways, it makes sense to mimic what other successful authors have done before you.

If you're the very first person past the post, or you have something new or original to add, then I take my hat off to you and so will everyone else. Such a step may also prove incredibly lucrative.

However, when too many others have trodden the path before you and the market is already overcrowded, then you are veering into the territory of cliché – a world of worn-out ideas which are starting to lose their impact. In this case, it may be time to rethink.

Can I Quote From Books, Songs or Poems Without Permission?

Authors often want to know whether they can use other people's copyrighted work within their own books – and whether they need to ask permission to include it.

I'd like to give some clarity on "permission" and copyright in this article. "Permission" means seeking permission to use someone else's copyrighted work in your own. In other words, you contact the copyright owner of the writing and ask permission to use the work. If the work is self-published, the copyright owner is the author. If the work is published by a publishing house, newspaper or magazine, then they will own the quotation rights rather than the writer.

Most publishers have a "permissions department" you can approach. They also have formal paperwork for you to sign that will detail the territories in which you have permission to use the copyrighted work. This will contain clauses detailing the conditions and any exceptions to the permission.

Sometimes, this permission is given for free as you are promoting and publicizing the other work. Often though, a fee is charged, which can range anywhere from a few dollars upwards to thousands of dollars.

Here are the exceptions when permission Is *not* needed:

- **Work in the public domain:** It can sometimes be hard to determine this. But as a rule of thumb, any work published before 1923 is considered to be in the public domain. There are also some works published after 1923 that are also in the public domain.

- **When mentioning only the title or author:** If you are just referring to the title of a work, stating a fact, you do not need permission.

- **"Fair use" guidelines:** If you only want to quote a few lines from a book, you are probably within fair use guidelines. You therefore are unlikely to need permission.

- **Creative Commons:** If a work is licensed under Creative Commons, no permission is required. This is usually prominently stated on the work itself, as an alternative to the copyright symbol. Many books, sites and blogs are licensed under Creative Commons.

It is important to remember that crediting the source of a work does *not* take away your obligation to seek permission. In fact, it is expected you should acknowledge your source regardless of fair use.

Fair Use in a Nutshell

There are four criteria for fair use, which is used mainly in US copyright and trademark law (the equivalent in the UK courts is "fair dealing"). These criteria are a little vague and therefore open to interpretation. Ultimately, it is up to the courts to make a final decision over what constitutes "fair use" when there is a disagreement.

The four criteria are:

1. The purpose and character of the use. Is the purpose of your work educational or for charity; or is it a commercial venture? If the main purpose of your work is to make money, this makes your case less sympathetic if you're borrowing a lot of someone else's copyrighted work.

2. The nature of the copyrighted work. Creative or imaginative works get the strongest protection. It is impossible to copyright a fact.

3. The size of the portion used compared to the entire quoted work. There is no percentage or word count suggested as a guideline by the courts. This is because some portions of a work may be considered to be the most valuable part or parts.

4. The effect on the potential market for or value of the quoted work. If using the original work damages the chances of people buying the original work, then you are violating fair use.

Copyright on Websites, Blogs, etc.

The same rules technically apply to copyrighted work online, but attitudes tend to be more relaxed. When bloggers use excerpts of copyrighted work (both from offline and online sources), it's more likely to be considered as "sharing" or "publicity" rather than as a violation of copyright. So you are bending the rules, but owners of the copyrighted work are less likely to pursue legal action.

Song Titles, TV Titles and Movie Titles

You do not need permission to include any kind of title in your work. It is OK to use: song titles, TV show titles, and movie titles without permission. You don't need permission to include the names of people, events, and places in your work. (Though if they are trademarked, that is another matter).

Song Lyrics and Poems

Because songs and poetry can be so short, it is best not to even include one line without asking for permission. This applies even if you think this could be considered fair use. It is OK to use the titles of songs or poems, and the names of bands or artists.

These are guidelines to help you, but it's always best to seek legal advice from a qualified lawyer as rules vary from territory to territory, and laws are constantly changing.

3 Tips to Avoid Distractions While You're Writing

Most writers feel overwhelmed at one point or another. In fact, staying focused can be one of the biggest daily challenges. There are always 101 other things that need doing – domestic, social and professional.

This can prevent you from getting your book written and published as quickly as you'd like. It quickly leads to that feeling of there never being enough hours in the day.

Here are some steps you can take to put yourself back on track:

1. **Focus on your results rather than your goals:** You might have a goal to complete your book by the end of the year. You may even have a series of mini-deadlines to help you achieve this. But what is the result you want? The result you want may be to get published, or to win an award, or to establish yourself as an expert. Writing your book is just part of the puzzle to achieve this. If you focus on your results, it helps you to see where you should be spending your time most effectively.

2. **Be specific:** Results need to be specific to be effective. "Do some writing" is not specific, for example. "Write 10 pages in the next week" is a very specific outcome. As is: "Redraft chapters 1 to 10 in the next 28 days." This is a much better way of monitoring your progress.

3. **Prioritize:** It's easy to get overwhelmed by the seemingly "urgent" tasks and lose sight of the truly important ones. Suppose you've bought a copy of the *Writers' Handbook*

and are wondering which agent to send your book to. But maybe you haven't written a pitch yet to achieve this outcome. Your first priority would therefore be to write an attention-grabbing pitch. That result would allow you to move on to your next goal of drawing up a shortlist of suitable literary agents. If you sent your book out too early, you'd probably end up with a pile of standard rejection letters. If you do things in the right order, it makes it so much easier to achieve results.

How To Write Your Book Faster

I often hear clients saying things like: "I just don't feel in the mood to write" or "I'm wondering if I'm writing the right book."

This stop-start problem is incredibly common even for experienced authors. Self-doubt starts to creep in, you get bored with your topic, or you start wondering if you could be writing a better book on a different topic.

What will help with this is to set aside thinking time and plan out your book before you start writing. I strongly encourage you to do this for any type of book. This is because it's so much easier to alter a one-page outline than a 300-page book if you suddenly decide your hero should be a heroine or that your book should be written in first person rather than third person!

Best-selling author, Jeffrey Archer, confided in me that he lies down on his bed for a while before starting his writing each day. This helps him to separate from his daily life and allows him to submerge in his fictional world.

It might feel slightly uncomfortable having "thinking time" as you may feel like you're doing "nothing" or may be keen to get cracking on with writing. But it really is worth setting aside time for planning before you get started and even when your book is underway.

You can plan out your book in a simple way using Post-it notes and a series of bullet points. Or you can do it more comprehensively. Barbara Taylor Bradford wrote a 100-page outline before she even started *A Woman of Substance*, for example. John Gray (author of *Men Are from Mars, Women Are from Venus*), on the other hand, told me that he always tries out his ideas for at least a year on his clients before putting them in his books. He also signs into Internet chat rooms, and tests his ideas anonymously!

Conflict is the motor that drives any plot. So, if at any point you are wondering why your plot has ground to a halt, just think of a fresh challenge for your characters or your reader to get the story rolling again. This can be a small internal challenge, such as a psychological conflict, or it can be a much more dramatic external conflict like a mysterious stranger or a destructive hurricane.

A similar principle applies to non-fiction books. If your plot grinds to a standstill, ask yourself: "What is the challenge that my reader needs to overcome?" and "How can I help them to overcome this?"

Try to set yourself a writing target each day, such as 1,000 words or 3,000 words. A standard book is approximately 70,000 words in length. So by setting yourself a daily target of say, 1,500 words, you will reach your goal in under 28 days. This will give you a solid first draft that you can then edit and re-edit to your satisfaction.

One of the wonderful things about breaking down a book into a 28-day writing plan is that the "impossible" suddenly seems much more achievable. You're not trying to tackle the mountain in one go, which would be exhausting. You have a clear strategy – with achievable daily goals – that will get you to where you want to be.

How To Choose A Bestselling Book Title

Introduction

What if you could sell ten times more books just by changing your title? Ok, that's believable. Are you sitting down? What if you could sell nearly a million more books just by changing your title?

No, this isn't hype. This is exactly what happened to author, Bob Morrison, when he self-published his book. When it first went on sale as *The Entrepreneurs' Manual* it sold only 12 copies. Disillusioned by these sales, and thinking the title needed an overhaul, he renamed it *Why S.O.B.s Succeed and Nice Guys Fail in Business*. The book has since sold over 800,000 copies.

Explosive results

In a world where we're bombarded with information, an attention-grabbing title can make all the difference between success and failure. If you're still having doubts, here's a handful of other manuscripts that have been successfully re-titled:

- *The Squash Book* was tested as a title versus *The Zucchini Cookbook*. The first title sold just 1,500 copies. The second sold 300,000 because it was more specific. It let people know exactly what it was about. It also addressed the needs of the many people who grow zucchini (or courgettes as they're know in the UK) and don't know what to do with them.

- Aspiring author, Colin McEnroe, created what he thought was a great book title, *Swimming Chickens*. After dismal sales, he decided to come up with another one. *Lose Weight Through Great Sex With Celebrities: The Elvis Way* went on to sell several hundred thousand copies.

- John Gray didn't get much attention with his book *What Your Mother Couldn't Tell You and What Your Father Didn't Know*. He shortened it to *Men are From Mars, Women are From Venus*. The rest, as they say, is history…

- The young F. Scott Fitzgerald sent his new novel, *Trimalchio in West Egg*, to publishers in 1924. Charles Scribner's Sons unsurprisingly hated the title and told him to change it. Fitzgerald obliged and came up with the bestseller, *The Great Gatsby*.

All very well and good, you might be thinking. But *how* do I go about choosing a good title?

How to choose a title

Top titles create anticipation, excitement and enthusiasm. They express the passion of your message. They connect emotionally with your reader. This then, is what you are aiming for.

Here are some tips to help you get started with both fiction and non-fiction titles:

1. Include 'How to' in your title.

How To Write A Bestseller / How to Become a Forex Trader

People love to learn with simple and easy steps. They like miracle solutions and 'quick fix' answers. In today's busy world, they like anything that suggests they can shave off time from their own learning curve.

2. Make a big promise.

Lose A Stone In Six Weeks / No More Sleepless Nights

If you have a big-gun promise, don't be afraid to use it. However, use your promise sparingly, and be ready to deliver. Your readers will remember if you fulfill your promises, and will come back for more. They'll also run a mile from hype ~ so give careful thought to what you're promising.

3. Command your readers.

Tame Your Toddler / Buy Your Dream Home in Brazil

The command has an immediate effect. It makes the reader think: "Yes, I want that!" It also reassures the reader that it's possible to achieve this and helpful advice will follow.

4. Offer your top benefit in your book title.

Think and Grow Rich / The 4-Hour Work Week

Winning non-fiction titles should tell the reader how they'll benefit from reading your book. What's the problem your book is going to solve? Readers buy books for something that will help them grow, profit, save money, improve health, or gain more time.

5. Ask a question.

When Did You Last See Your Father? / Who Stole My Church? / How Good Is Your Sex Life?

Most times. your reader will answer your question in their

minds. They'll be hooked in. The key is providing the answers in your book.

6. Be provocative.

So You Don't Want To Go To Church Any More? / Don't Waste Your Life

Provocative statements jolt our attention like electric shocks. They make us curious. They make us angry. Most of all, they make us want to read on.

7. Use 'key words'.

Secrets of the Millionaire Mind / Bend It Like Beckham.

Key words grab reader's attention. However, in the Internet age, here's another good reason why they're important. If you're planning to sell your book online, it'll help readers to locate your book via subject searches on sites like Amazon.

8. Be outrageous.

Sex in a Tent / The Nigger Factory

Take a risk. Write without fear of judgment or prejudice. Break boundaries. Challenge taboos. Make people sit up and take notice.

9. Use words that intrigue or arouse curiosity.

The Life & Loves of a She Devil / The Man Who Mistook His Wife For A Hat

Books and films offer escapism and fantasy. They provide a chance to experience larger-than-life characters and experiences. Any title that hints at a life less ordinary is bound to arouse curiosity and interest.

10. Use pictures or strong visual images to provoke your audience.

Miss Smilla's Feeling For Snow / The Colour Purple / A Thousand Splendid Suns

Use the strong words, colours, or sensory images to stir your audience's imagination. Use a picture or metaphor to get started.

11. Use alliteration, rhyme or repetition.

What to Expect When You're Expecting / How Much Poo Does An Elephant Do?

People respond to words or phrases that are catchy and memorable. This is why pensioners can still recite the nursery rhymes they learned when they were toddlers! It's why you can find yourself singing along to jingles, TV ads or pop music even though they irritate you! Love 'em or hate 'em, they stick in your head.

Try testing titles on your friends and family, then pick the one that does best. You'll be a lot closer to sales success than by just guessing.

Your title may end up being only be one word long. However it's worth devoting considerable time and energy to getting it right. Remember that many authors and publishers have used this knowledge before you, to turn sales disasters into phenomenal success stories! Your efforts can be rewarded in the same way too...

How To Find A Publisher Or Literary Agent For Your Book

Feedback on your fiction or non-fiction book can sometimes be confusing or even conflicting.

A complaint I often hear is that several literary agents or editors are giving very different advice, so whose advice should you listen to if you want to get published? For example, an author recently wrote to me saying that two different publishers had read and rejected the manuscript for his debut crime thriller.

Publisher A rejected the book, saying the plot was too complex. Publisher B identified various subplots to be removed if they were to publish the book, saying that the manuscript was too long. However, once this had been done, the author was then told that the plot was "too thin".

He wrote: "This has left me a little confused. Now with two versions, and two opinions, I'm not sure how best to improve and move the novel forward before resubmitting elsewhere."

Here are my thoughts, which I hope will help you if you're in a similar position, whether you are writing fiction or non-fiction.

First of all, to get *any* publisher or literary agent to read your manuscript is extremely positive and means that your manuscript is marketable. This alone is a very encouraging sign. Many publishers and agents receive over 200 manuscripts per week and some of the biggest publishing names receive over 200 manuscripts per day. They certainly will not read your book if they do not think it has promise. They simply don't have the time or resources.

Yes, it can be very subjective how editors and literary agents respond to a novel or non-fiction book. However, bear in mind that all publishers have a different "house style". You can think of this as a brand or unique hallmark that differentiates them from each other.

So, first of all, check if they are actually reading your book. If you are getting lots of generic rejection letters – these are usually very vague and don't refer to anything specific in your plot – then the chances are that your manuscript has not been read. If so, then your covering letter and pitch probably isn't strong enough.

If this is the case, then you need to go away and work on writing a more compelling and attention-grabbing submission letter and synopsis.

If, on the other hand, editors and agents are reading your manuscript, then you need to determine whether they are simply asking you to adapt your book to their particular house style or brand. This can make sense of what otherwise seem like contradictory comments. Suppose you've written an historical romance for example. A publisher of historical books and costume dramas is likely to ask you to include more period detail. Whereas a publisher such as Mills & Boon, will ask you to focus on the love scenes.

Consider if you are getting the same feedback consistently. For example, several publishers may tell you that your opening chapter is weak. Or several agents may say that there is insufficient conflict in your plot. If this is the case, it may be time to give your manuscript a rewrite.

You can do this with the help of a literary consultancy service or a writer's coach. Many manuscript assessment services will give you an objective opinion on your book. This will involve an 8 to 12-page report giving feedback on your manuscript, highlighting the strengths and weaknesses, as well as making constructive suggestions for improvements.

This can make an enormous difference in fine-tuning your writing before you begin submitting you manuscript again.

My Literary Agent Can't Sell My Book – What Should I Do?

So you've been signed up with a literary agent. They've had your manuscript for 18 months. They've sent it to a dozen publishers. But they still can't get you a book deal. Now they're saying maybe you should write another book and put the current one on hold for now. What should you do?

Before you make a decision, set up a meeting or phone call with your agent to discuss the situation. You may be irate, but it's important not to let this show. Record the meeting on your mobile if necessary. It's vital that you hear what they have to say and understand where they are coming from.

Questions you might ask are:

- Why isn't my book selling?
- Is there anything I can do to make my book more marketable?
- Is it worth rewriting my book?
- Can I see publishers' feedback?

Afterward, ask yourself: "Does what s/he is saying resonate with me?" For example, if your agent says your book is out of date, have you had this sneaking suspicion all along? If they say your plot is too weak, do you agree? You can also ask for a second opinion from a publishing professional or a literary consultancy before making a final decision.

After weighing things up, you may agree with what they say. You may decide to stay put and pour your energies into writing a new book.

On the other hand, you may disagree. You may feel it's too much of a risk to write another book, knowing you could face the exactly same situation in the future. In this case, you may decide to represent yourself.

A lot of writers are understandably reluctant about representing themselves. However, there are hundreds of publishers in the world. These include the small independent presses that most literary agents won't even look at. Just because a dozen publishers have rejected your book doesn't mean everyone will.

Self-publishing is also a viable option that has made best sellers of many supposedly "unpublishable" books. There are so many self-publishing options these days: print-on-demand, e-books, "hybrid" publishing.

Finally, believe in yourself. Take heart from the fact that a literary agent took you on in the first place. Agents are busy people. They send your book out at their own expense. They really wouldn't give you the time of day if they didn't think you had talent!

"All Publishers Are Idiots!"

Imagine walking up to a stranger in the street ... and asking for $1,000.

"I'm going to the races," you say. "When I come back I'll have doubled or even tripled your money. Hell, I might even surprise you and make a cool million."

Do you think he or she is going to hand over the money? Erm. Tough one, but probably not.

OK, this is the type of letter that I occasionally receive in my mailbox and I never know whether to laugh or cry:

"What is wrong with the publishing industry is they are stale, they won't take a chance with none published writers. I have never had a bad letter about my writings only (enjoyed your book good luck) or words to that effect. If they enjoy my stories (children's stories) why not take a chance!?!"

Shall I answer or would you like to?

Why do publishers and agents reject books? Hmm. Tricky.

What About Writer's Block?

What about writer's block? What do you do on days when you feel less inspired than usual?

Well, I'm not a big fan of "writer's block". It smacks too much of "can't do" for my liking. I've never been one for letting things hold me back – life is far too short.

So consider this. What if you don't feel like getting out of bed in the morning? Or if you don't feel like taking your kids to school? Or if you don't feel like going to work or speaking to your clients?

Of course there are going to be times when we feel less vibrant, less energetic, less inspired than others. But it is essential to keep going. It's important to keep writing – even if it's for only 30 minutes per day – no matter whether you're feeling inspired or uninspired.

Treat your writing as a "job" rather than a hobby. If you're feeling particularly stuck try a change of scenery. Write in a different room. Or if you're used to sitting in front of your keyboard, try using voice recognition software or a dictaphone so that you speak your words.

Treat your "block" as a temporary challenge that you intend to blast through. Before long, you'll find that same creative spark is glowing bright again.

Should I Self-Publish My Non-Fiction Book or is a Mainstream Publisher Better?

Writers often wonder: "Should I self-publish my non-fiction book or is a mainstream publisher better?"

To help you with this decision, I recommend that you first of all think about how you are intending to promote and market your book. Who are your target readers? Why would they want to buy your book? What is unique and special about it? Do you have any ideas for promoting and marketing your book, both online and offline?

What many new authors don't realise is that mainstream publishers tend to be distributors rather than marketers. After you've signed on the dotted line, you suddenly discover that you still have to do all the public relations (PR) and marketing yourself – and then, to rub salt into the wound, you have to hand over a large percentage of your royalties!

So here are the questions you really must ask yourself before making any final decision:

1. **What do you know about PR and marketing?** If you don't know much about PR and marketing, then are you willing to learn? Are you willing to spend the time relentlessly promoting your book both before and after its launch? Or can you afford to pay someone else to do this for you?

2. **Can you sell your book?** Do you have a mailing list or database of people you could sell your book to? These might be your connections on LinkedIn, Facebook or

Twitter. Or they might be subscribers to your blog. If you're a businessperson or a professional, do you have a client list or newsletter you can use?

3. **Can you persuade someone else to sell your book?** If you don't have a "list" of your own, can you think of anyone else who might help you? If you've written a book about childbirth, then midwives or health visitors might be good people to approach. If you've written a book about diet, can you promote it via fitness centres or gyms? Or can you approach HR departments with your book about workplace bullying?

4. **Do you want to create other products from the same content?** Do you want to repurpose your work so that it appears as different products in different formats? You might want to produce a home-study course and an audio series with the same content as your book. This can sometimes be the clincher as many mainstream publishers have a clause in their contract that prohibits this.

5. **Is this your passion?** Finally, the most important question of all: does this make your heart sing? Self-publishing a book can bring amazing rewards for authors. However, it *is* hard work. If you don't love selling your book, if your heart isn't in it, then self-publishing definitely won't be for you.

To conclude, the answer is different for everyone. Some writers will be lousy at self-publishing. Others – usually, those of an entrepreneurial nature – will be most likely be frustrated and held back by the restrictions of mainstream publishing. By answering the above questions, you should be able to work out the best solution for you.

The Difference Between Vanity Publishing and Self-Publishing

I just had to write about this topic as it concerns a publishing ruse all writers should be aware of. I certainly wasn't aware of this before no, so I'm sure it will catch some of you by surprise too. I have to say that I nearly fell off my chair when I heard about it.

A first-time novelist has just sent their book to what they thought was a publishing house. The publisher told them their book wasn't of a high enough standard for their list. However, it was suitable for self-publishing with their sister company at a cost of … drum roll … £10,000 for just over 100 books.

Are they mad? Do they really think writers will fall for this? Obviously not all that mad, because the writer who told me about this had already agreed to pay this sum.

Please, please, please do your research before considering anything so drastic. Most printing companies are charging in the region of £2,500 per 1,000 books. That's around £2.50 per book. If you want a larger print run, then you'll be paying even less. And with print-on-demand, you'll only be paying for books on a copy by copy basis.

It's easy to feel disheartened and crushed when you've had one too many rejections. Yes, you can feel like you're never going to reach your goal. But there really is no need to go reaching for your credit card when you're offered a "solution" that costs £10,000.

If you're having no luck getting your book published, then learn about marketing, get a mentor, rewrite your book, have someone check over your pitch. Look at independent publishing houses or take a serious look at self-publishing.

Self-publishing is not – most definitely *not* – a "second best" these days. For many authors, it can actually be a better option than a mainstream publisher. £10,000 for a handful of books is vanity publishing, not self-publishing. You and your book deserve far better than this.

A large number of my clients have earned over six figures – and even seven figures – from savvy self-publishing. Notice that I say *savvy* self-publishing. This doesn't mean randomly self-publishing a book or e-book, then putting it on Amazon, using the "hope and pray" method.

It means having a proper strategy before you launch your book into the marketplace. It means having a proper marketing plan and PR timeline, that you then stick to. There are no shortcuts with this – even when you're published by a mainstream publishing house, you'll still be expected to promote your book.

Having spent time and effort writing your book, surely this is no less than it deserves? One of the great joys of self-publishing is that the rewards are linked to the amount of effort that you put in. What's more, you won't be earning a measly 10-20% royalties that you'd get from a mainstream publisher.

Why Some Authors Are "Luckier" Than Others!

I was wondering how to motivate one of my clients to finish his book, as life and work seemed to keep getting in his way. So I recklessly said: "Let's have a bet: let's see if you can finish your book before I write mine."

Before I knew it, we'd agreed that I'd roll up my sleeves and clean his car, inside and out, if he succeeded in finishing first.

I had no ideas for a book at that stage. However, the Number 1 question many of my clients were asking me was: "How do I sell a million books?" And so, *Celebrity Authors' Secrets: Tips from Famous Authors Who Were Once Unknown* was conceived.

It was easy enough to identify authors who'd sold over a million books. In fact, I'd worked with many of them during my years working as a literature adviser for The Arts Council of England. So I set myself the goal of finishing my book within four weeks and launching it to coincide with a big publishing conference I was hosting in London in the autumn.

Everything seemed to be going smoothly at the start. "This bet is going to be a doddle," I thought. Never mind that my client owned a dog that shed copious amounts of fur and left muddy pawprints on his upholstery. I only had about 10 hours of interviews to do, and maybe another 2 hours writing the introduction. I was looking forward to my people carrier having a good clean after so many school runs with my kids.

Except that I started hitting unexpected snags …

I contacted over 100 best-selling authors and their agents,

requesting interviews. But, to begin with, no-one wanted to talk to me. They either didn't reply, were too busy, or sent polite rejections. Or, in a handful of cases, they were rather rude!

Authors I approached included:

- J. K. Rowling
- Dan Brown
- Jacqueline Wilson
- Danielle Steel
- John Grisham
- James Patterson
- Bill Bryson
- Patricia Cornwell
- Ian Rankin
- Julia Donaldson
- Francesca Simon
- Martina Cole
- Philip Pullman
- Stephenie Meyer
- Delia Smith
- Stephen King
- Marian Keyes
- Josephine Cox
- Sophie Kinsella
- Jodi Picoult
- Terry Deary
- Anthony Horowitz
- Ian McEwan
- Wilbur Smith
- Sebastian Faulks
- Helen Fielding
- Lee Child
- Dave Pelzer
- Mark Haddon
- Joanna Trollope
- Jackie Collins
- Louis de Bernières

- Jack Higgins
- Anita Shreve
- Robert Harris
- Frank McCourt
- Salman Rushdie
- Robert Allen
- Anthony Robbins
- Louise Hay
- Lynne Truss
- Robert Kiyosaki
- Bob Proctor
- Deepak Chopra
- Brian Tracy
- Marianne Williamson
- Mark Victor Hansen
- Malcolm Gladwell
- Khaled Hosseini
- Ken Follett
- Tim Ferris
- Eckhart Tolle
- Marci Shimoff
- Joe Vitale

Eventually though, I started to get some traction. The late Terry Pratchett phoned me 10 minutes after receiving my email saying that he wanted to be interviewed there and then. I hadn't had time to prepare: I hadn't researched his books, I hadn't compiled a list of interview questions, I hadn't even set up my recording equipment. But he had a busy timetable writing his own book: so it was one of those now or never moments. It wasn't the best interview I've ever done in my career as a journalist. But at least I had one author "in the bag" as it were.

Terry was rapidly followed by Jeffrey Archer, author of *Kane and Abel* who was a bit of a flirt, and peppered his conversation with "you wicked woman!" My editor later had much fun deleting this, and I also got to visit him at his apartment alongside The Thames in London.

I started to get on a roll then. John Gray, author of *Men Are from Mars, Women Are from Venus* followed. Then, others rapidly fell into place: Joanne Harris (*Chocolat*); Barbara Taylor Bradford (*A Woman of Substance*); James Redfield (*The Celestine Prophecy*); Anne Rice (*Interview with the Vampire*) and Eric Carle (*The Hungry Caterpillar*). All so helpful, nice, and surprisingly down-to-earth.

Eventually, there were 12 authors, all of whom had sold over a million books. But my point is this: around 10 per cent of the people I contacted agreed to be interviewed. I was rejected by at least 90. The book took much longer to write than anticipated: it took nearly a year to write and wasn't published until the following spring.

Most people reading my book won't know the background to it. They'll see the big names and think I drew on my contacts as a BBC and IRN newsreader or my Oxford University contacts. Nope. I cold-called a lot of them. Some knew me, yes. But most of them had absolutely no idea who I was and couldn't have cared less. I was just willing to put myself out there, to face embarrassment, rejection and disappointment.

When I was small, my mother frequently told me the fable of "The Tortoise and the Hare". If you've never read it before, it's a story of how persistence and determination allows a slow tortoise to win a race – even when the competition (the hare) is a much faster sprinter. Mum often reminded me in all areas of my life: "What matters is that you keep plodding on until the very end and never give up. Often, it's the plodders who are the winners – not those who are fastest or cleverest!"

That lesson always stuck with me: that persistence and determination often win the day. You have to believe in yourself even when others don't. You have to keep going even when you don't seem to be getting anywhere. If you discover a challenge or obstacle blocking your way, you find a way around it.

The best thing of all was that my client eventually did finish his book and get it published. Then, surprisingly and amazingly, he turned into a publishing super-whizz. He churned out 5 new books in a matter of months, one after the other. He also started hosting events with £500 tickets, and selling them out.

So did I have to roll up my sleeves, grab a sponge, and get covered in soap suds and dog hairs? No, thankfully his first book was the slowest of them all.

Maybe another time with a different client ... I'm always open to a fresh challenge!

How to Choose the Right Literary Agent For Your Book

A literary agent is one of the best ways to accelerate your progress as a successful author. Most peoples simply don't have the global publishing contacts to sell their work. Even if they did, they wouldn't know how to negotiate a book deal or a publishing contract.

But how do you find a literary agent, and how do you choose the right one? Here are six simple tips to help you:

1. Research your agent

Get hold of a copy of the *Writers' Handbook* which lists every literary agent in the USA and UK. (You can get these in most book stores and libraries.) Most of the literary agents list the writers they represent – ideally these authors should be writing in a similar genre to you. Check on the agents' specialist areas. (There's no point sending a military book to someone who specializes in sci-fi!) Draw up a shortlist of potential candidates. Another way to select agents is to flick through similar books to yours in a bookstore. Most authors credit their agents on their acknowledgments page, so this should give you a good idea of likely candidates.

2. Target your agents

Check out the agents' websites. Where possible, personalize your letters and use first names. It's labour-intensive and likely to take more of your time. However, it will reap rewards as your letter is less likely to get intercepted by the gatekeepers (aka PAs and secretaries!) who are sometimes geared to sending out generic rejections. Target agents where you will obviously fit in with other authors on their list. A scattergun strategy is less effective than one that's precisely targeted.

3. Big agency?

Decide from the outset what you'd like from your working relationship with an agent. With a bigger agency, you're going to be a small fish in a big pond. If your agent has a conflicting engagement tying in with Madonna's book or yours, it's easy to guess which one will be cancelled! (And yes, this *did* actually happen to me with a literary agent many years ago!) At times, your working relationship can seem very impersonal and businesslike. However, a larger agency is likely to have a big film rights department and foreign rights department with a team of staff all working hard to sell your book around the world. This leverages your time enormously as you have the weight of a big team behind you.

4. Small agency?

There are plenty of one-man (and one-woman) bands. The lovely thing about these smaller agencies is that they often have a very warm and friendly working relationship with writers on their list. If you're a new author who'd like a bit of hand-holding and detailed feedback, then a smaller agency may be ideal. Smaller agencies tend to outsource foreign rights and film rights work to other agencies. The main disadvantage is that there are usually only one or two people handling all the clients. If your agent is away at the Frankfurt Book Fair or off on holiday, this can leave you feeling high and dry.

5. Medium agency?

Medium-sized agencies tend to be my favourites. These agencies offer the best of both worlds. They have foreign rights and film departments. Yet they are not so big that you feel lost in them. You can often arrive at a medium-sized agency and find that pretty much everyone there has read your book right the way through to the PA and the office secretary!

6. Prepare questions

Meet an agent before you sign with them to make sure your aims align with theirs. I constantly meet authors who complain about their literary agents, even detest them. You'll be having a close, and hopefully long, working relationship with your agent. It's essential that you choose someone who you feel is on the same wavelength.

How to Annoy Literary Agents

Writers and authors often wonder how many literary agents they should submit to at one time. Faced with a cut-throat publishing environment, it's tempting to try to speed up the process by sending a mass mail-out.

I recently heard of one writer who submitted to 200 literary agents in one go. Yes, 200! This reeks of desperation, as well as a total lack of confidence, in both your pitch and your book.

If your pitch and manuscript are strong enough to attract a literary agent's or publisher's attention, then you only need to send it to three or four agents at a time. Or, if you're really impatient, to a dozen at most.

Sending a pitch randomly to several hundred agents is *not* the way to go.

First of all, it will wind them up enormously if word gets out – for example, during the week of The Frankfurt Book Fair when many agents mingle socially. Secondly, should you really be sending out your pitch if you're that uncertain about it?

On the other hand, if you believe, hand on heart, that you have a fantastic pitch, do you really want to print 200 manuscripts and send them to 200 literary agents when the feeding frenzy begins? Is that really the best way to spend your precious time?

What all writers should be aiming for is precision marketing. That means a precise and targeted campaign where you have maximized your chances with a killer pitch and a submission letter that hits them right between the eyes. This way, you are confident of getting results before you even start out.

If you find yourself thinking of a random spray gun approach, then something is seriously wrong. Get your pitch right *before* you send it out to literary agents. It is no good crossing your fingers and hoping for the best.

Understand what they are looking for, what will sell in the market, and then deliver. Read books, attend seminars, get a mentor, and learn as much as you can. This is what will open doors for you.

Red Flags to Watch Out for in Your Publishing Contract – What Authors Unwittingly Sign Away

The antics of some publishers never cease to amaze me. What makes me gasp even harder is that most authors – even experienced ones – are oblivious to what they're unwittingly signing away.

In the euphoria of finally getting a book deal, many authors overlook the fact that they are getting rather a raw deal in their publishing contract. This naiveté prevents them from getting deals that are better for them and better for their books.

I was recently reading a publishing contract for one of my clients. He's a prominent celebrity, at the top of his field, and regularly featured on TV.

Here are some of the things that I flagged up, before he signed on the dotted line:

World Rights and Film Rights

In one fell swoop, the author was signing away his UK rights, world rights, TV rights, digital rights, and film rights, to name but a few. All for the grand sum of – wait for it – £5,000.

Most literary agents will sell your UK rights, your American rights, your Australian rights, etc. separately. They'll also sell your film option as a separate deal. If any publisher suggests you hand over all rights, make damn well sure you are paid a decent sum for it.

Something else to bear in mind: you need to be certain the publisher is actually going to do something with these rights. Ideally, there must be a clause committing to some sort of definite action – otherwise your manuscript could easily end up gathering dust in a forgotten drawer.

Break Clause

What if there is a strong demand for your book, but your publisher decides not to reprint it? Or what if it is remaindered, but you can't persuade them that your genre is suddenly fashionable again? Or supposing, many years after your death, one of your descendants would like to publish your out-of-print work?

A break clause allows the rights to revert to the author after a certain period – usually three years after a book has been remaindered or goes out of print. It ensures that a publisher does not retain the rights indefinitely.

Competition Cause

As most successful authors know, the big money is in the upsell. In other words, higher-priced products – such as home study courses, CD sets, DVD sets – which are spin-off products from your book.

If you are planning to repurpose or rewrite your content and sell other similar products, beware "competition" clauses that tie your hands. This is particularly relevant when it comes to non-fiction books.

Options On Subsequent Books

Many times, publishers request the option to consider the author's next book before it is shown to any other publisher. The author is so thrilled and flattered by this that they overlook the fact that this isn't necessarily best for them or their book.

Sure, if a publisher pays for this option, that's great. But if it's just a clause in your contract that commits you to offering them first refusal on your next book, without any commitment to accept it, this just ties your hands. It's a rather one-way deal!

Print Run

Ideally, your book contract will specify an exact print run for your book. Many publishers will print 3,000 books and think that this is a good print run. Others will print 35,000 books. In rare instances, the number will run into millions. Unless you know this figure, the royalties percentages in your book contract are meaningless.

Deadline

Make sure there is a realistic deadline for your book. My client was committed to a two-month deadline to complete a 60,000-word book. He planned to take two months off to write it. Had he ever written a book in such a short time frame before, I asked? "No," was the answer. This ridiculously tight deadline again favoured the publisher, but left the author little leeway for rewrites and changes of plan. As a rule of thumb, give an estimate for the length of time it will take to write your book, then double it!

Publication Date

The launch date for a book is an important part of marketing. Dieting books are much more likely to sell in January when everyone is making New Year resolutions, for example. Horror books sell better around Halloween.

Ideally, your book contract will contain a specific publication date, which shows that some thought and effort has been put into the marketing of your book.

Marketing and PR

I've lost count of the number of disillusioned authors who complain to me about their publisher's lousy (or complete lack of) marketing and PR for their books. It is rare indeed to find clauses in book contracts committing to a specific budget for marketing and PR strategies. However, if you can get a sum agreed in your contract, you know that your publisher is serious and committed – and your book will stand a much better chance of success.

This is just a brief overview of things to look out for in your book contract – especially if you are going it alone and negotiating without a literary agent. Weigh up your options and consider every clause carefully.

After working with me, my client was able to go back to his publisher and negotiate a much better deal by deleting some clauses and asking for others to be inserted.

After spending so much time and effort writing your book, don't be too speedy in signing your rights away!

What Do Publishers' Rejection Letters *Really* Mean?

You've been waiting on tenterhooks for an agent or publisher to get back to you about your book. Now you have the letter – but you're wondering exactly what it means. Often, there's so little information given in a rejection letter that you're left confused about how to decipher it.

Does this agent really like my book? Does the publisher hate it? Have they bothered to read it at all? You're left to make your own judgement – but 9 times out of 10, writers get this wrong.

To take away the guesswork, here is a quick guide to what letters might say and what they probably mean.

1. *"We regret we're unable to take on any new writers."* Exactly that. Have they read your pitch? Probably not. They're deluged with manuscripts and just too overwhelmed with work.

2. *"Your synopsis and opening chapter have promise, but we already have a similar author on our list."* You are right to feel encouraged. They can see the potential in your work. You just haven't found the right person to represent you yet.

3. *"I enjoyed reading your full manuscript. I just don't feel passionate enough about it to represent you."* High praise indeed. Agents and publishers are rushed off their feet and don't give praise lightly. They certainly wouldn't bother reading a manuscript unless they thought it was publishable.

4. ***"The plot wasn't compelling enough. The narrative was plodding."*** Thank them for their frankness and honesty. Time for a rewrite or a second opinion!

Rejection can sting at times. But remember that many famous writers faced rejection in their early years. Louisa May Alcott, Beatrix Potter, Agatha Christie, and George Orwell are among them. So have faith in yourself and your abilities – and keep going!

Your Book Can Be a Massive Bestseller – Even If Publishers Have Rejected It!

So your book's been rejected by an agent or publisher? Take heart! For many authors, rejection is the very catalyst that springboards them to success.

Here are some awe-inspiring true stories to show you what can be achieved with a little faith and courage. I've been selective here, but I could have easily filled an entire book with authors' success stories. I hope these writers will inspire you as much as they do me:

- Screenwriter Kenya Cagle went to the Cannes Film Festival in an attempt to cold-sell a script written 15 years previously. He had sent *The Undercover Man* out to more than 100 movie studios. Not one responded. When he came home from Cannes in 2001, he had a $5 million production deal.

- Professional wildlife photographers Carl Sams and Jean Stoick achieved bestseller status for a book they were told would never sell. Today, there are more than a million copies of *Stranger in the Woods* in print. It's won seven awards and spent 26 weeks on the *New York Times* bestseller list.

- Paul Tawrell believed so much in his book that he sold his house and paid a Canadian printer $125,000 for 35,000 copies. This proved a brilliant move. *Camping & Wilderness Survival* sold over 320,000 copies.

- After rejections from 26 publishers, Vicki Stringer self-published her novel using donations from family and friends. *Let That Be the Reason* sold 1,000 copies from her car boot in the first three weeks. By 2005, her estimated sales leaped to 1.8 million! She now publishes 16 other authors.

- Fantasy novel *Eragon* catapulted its teenage author to stardom after it was self-published. After over a year selling his book from town to town, Christopher Paolini finally received a six-figure deal for the novel and two sequels. The novel has since been made into a film starring Jeremy Irons.

- Vicky Lansky's children's recipe book, *Feed Me, I'm Yours*, was rejected by 49 publishers. It sold 300,000 copies after being self-published. After Bantam took it over, it sold 8 million more! Vicky now has more than 30 books to her credit and a very successful small press.

I've used only a handful of examples. Yet, there are thousands more writers who have achieved similar success. To quote film director, George Lucas: "In my experience, there's no such thing as luck." Anyone who is committed will create their own good fortune.

Never give up – even when things seem to be going badly for you. Rejection is just one step in your journey, not the end of it.

Will Publishers Accept or Reject Your Book?

Are you killing your chances stone dead before your book even lands on an agent's or publisher's desk? You probably are, though you may not realise it.

It's no secret that publishing has changed over the past decade or so. In the past, most readers bought their paperbacks and hardbacks from book stores, and big publishers had a stranglehold on the market. Nowadays, many people buy their books online and many book stores have closed.

To combat the changes, publishing houses are increasingly led by sales teams with commercial aims. Literary agents have had to adopt these values too. So authors have to develop new tactics to keep abreast of the changes. If you don't, you won't survive in this unforgiving climate.

If you keep getting rejection letters, it's time to time to change your methods and learn new skills. Here are some of the typical mistakes that even professional authors make when pitching their books:

1. Forgetting Your Reader

If a publishing house is going to the expense of printing your book, they want to know they'll be able to sell it. It will help you no end if you can show them why your book is going to sell and who they are going to sell it to. What is special about your book? Who is likely to buy it? Why should they choose your book rather than someone else's?

2. Weak Sales Pitch

Most authors fail to flag up the key selling points for their books. They sometimes use jargon or academic language that only appeals to a small minority.

Try to make your synopsis and introductory letter as accessible as possible. Put some sparkle into your pitch to arouse curiosity or engage interest. If there's a best-selling book that's similar to yours, point this out.

3. Uninspiring Synopsis

Your synopsis is probably the most important page you're going to write. Get this wrong and you won't even be allowed on the starting block, let alone run the race. Put twice as much effort into your synopsis as any other page in your book. Check out the blurbs of best sellers to get help you get this right.

4. Long-winded Submission Letter

Publishers and agents are busy people. They don't have time to read a long introductory letter detailing your professional career, or telling them that your friends all love your book.

Your submission letter should ideally be no longer than two pages of double-spaced A4. If you can make it shorter than this, even better.

5. Dull Sample Chapters

Imagine yourself in a room filled with thousands of books. All these books have white covers. There's little to distinguish them. How would you choose the best one? Would you read every book cover-to-cover, patiently waiting for the plot to unfold? Or would you skim through the opening pages, tossing aside anything that seemed too dull or ordinary?

Start your book with something startling, memorable, or original. This can be a challenge, a question, or a crisis. Grab the reader's attention. Make them want to keep turning the pages.

6. Poor Layout and Presentation

Publishers don't want single-spaced pages in 10-point typeface. They don't want fancy fonts or coloured paper. You may think it will grab their attention. It will, but for all the wrong reasons.

Use double-spacing and 12-point typeface. Number your pages and include a word count. Put your book title at the top of every page. This will ensure your manuscript looks professional and businesslike.

7. Sending Out Work Before It's Ready

If you send your book out before it's ready, you'll end up doing yourself more harm than good.

Make sure someone with a credible reputation has read your manuscript before you post it. If possible, get a professional endorsement. This means finding a reputable author or editor to read your book. You can then quote their comments as part of your pitch.

8. Getting Bogged Down By Small Detail

Often when writers revise their books, they focus on deleting sentences or tweaking paragraphs. They change colons to hyphens, and full stops to commas. They get swamped in the small detail.

When revising your manuscript, remember the bigger picture. Ask yourself: is there enough drama or intrigue? Are there enough challenges, conflicts or questions? Are your chapters logically structured? Do you open your book with a bang rather than a whimper? It's plot and emotional connection that sells a book, rather than grammar and punctuation!

9. Pestering

There's a fine line between pestering and perseverance. Writers sometimes forget that agents are giving their services for free up until the moment that a book is sold. This means they're covering the considerable costs for staff, time and paperwork, with their own money. This is a tremendous privilege, not an automatic right.

Making a nuisance of yourself by hassling agents – or publishers – is unlikely to result in anything positive. No matter how frustrated you feel, make sure you're always pleasant and polite.

If you're making any of the mistakes I've mentioned, take heart. It's something that can be fixed. These simple marketing tricks can help you create a pitch that will have agents and publishers clamouring to read your book. You may even be taken on by someone who has previously rejected you.

An Agent Or Publisher Has Rejected Your Book – Why it Pays to Keep Going

It's the classic catch 22. Most publishers won't look at your manuscript unless you have an agent. And some literary agents won't read your book unless you have a publisher. Rejection letters seem to be dropping through your letterbox every other day. You're just about ready to give up.

In over 20 years of working with writers, there's something I've noticed about the most successful of them. It isn't talent that differentiates them. They have something way more important than the words they write. They have a persistence and tenacity that sees them through the hurdles.

Over eighty per cent of people say they want to write a book. But not many of them have the perseverance to see it through. As with most things, it's about mindset. If you want to succeed, you need an unshakable self-belief at your core. Having the right mindset is far more valuable than the words you set down on the page.

Ignore everything you read in the media – genuine stories of "instant fame" and "meteoric success" are few and far between. Many of the big names in writing have served long apprenticeships before achieving fame and fortune. Joanna Trollope must have had steam coming out of her ears when she told a journalist that it had taken her 20 years to become an "overnight sensation". Author Philip Pullman CBE echoed the sentiment when he told a BBC reporter: "It took me 30 years to become an overnight success." Similarly, Mark Haddon was a writer and illustrator for 16 years before *The Curious Incident of the Dog in the Night-Time* won the Whitbread Award in

2003. His five attempts at writing an adult novel are still languishing in a drawer, at the time of writing.

Unfortunately, *Shoots to Fame after Years of Hard Slog* does not make a good newspaper headline!

I've known many talented authors – writers of brilliant and scintillating prose – over the years who have fallen by the wayside. It wasn't their talent or ability that let them down. It was simply that they didn't have the staying power to keep going. They didn't have the ability to bounce back from rejection or the flexibility to learn from mistakes. Or their negative attitude meant that they were their own worst enemy. They had opportunities that would have been the envy of many other writers. Yet, they spent so much time moaning and complaining that publishers or agents eventually dropped them from their lists.

If you want to be a success as a writer, then work on your mindset. Find the unshakable self-belief at your core. Develop a resilience and tenacity. Develop "out-of-the-box" thinking. If Plan A or Plan B doesn't work, then train yourself to think about plans C, D, and E. This will help you when nothing's going the way it's supposed to.

Because you know what? If someone says "no" or "it's not possible", you'll get twice the pleasure when you prove them wrong!

Publication Day – The Most Disappointing Day Of Your Life?

I was chatting to a senior commissioning editor at a publishing house recently. "What we really *should* be telling authors is that the day their book comes out will probably be one of the most disappointing days of their life," he said.

Why did he say this – when publication is considered the "pinnacle" of success for so many writers, especially when it's publication by a prominent publishing house?

Sadly, for many authors, traditional publishing is a huge anti-climax. Amidst all the hype about getting a book published, this is something that's rarely talked about openly. This is because many authors, when they hand over their manuscript, also hand over responsibility for marketing and PR of their book. They may be hoping for lots of reviews in mainstream media or a flurry of readings. But these don't always materialize.

Too often these days, I hear from disillusioned authors who feel that their editor or agent has done "next to nothing" to publicize their book. Or they don't like the marketing angle or the genre chosen by the marketing team.

The solution? Take matters into your own hands at least three months before publication date.

- Compile a list of people to send review copies to.
- Write your own press release and get interviews on national and local media.
- Leave posts about your book on relevant online forums.

- If you haven't done it already, contact celebrities to get endorsements for your book.

- Learn as much about marketing and PR as you can – and apply it.

- Write a blog or set up a Facebook author page.

- Organize a virtual book tour.

- Give away sample chapters or free reports to mailing lists that are likely to be interested in your subject matter.

In short, create hype and excitement in the run-up to your launch.

Your book is *your* baby. No one else is going to love it, nurture it, or cherish it like you do. So never leave the responsibility for promoting your book in someone else's hands, even if they *are* a big publishing house.

Make sure your publication date is a day of excitement and celebration – the big event it deserves to be.

How to Write a Marketing Plan or Your Book

Many writers are taken by surprise when they receive a request for a detailed marketing plan – often before an agent or publisher has even taken them on. Don't be daunted. Treat this as an opportunity rather than a hurdle. Increasingly, agents and publishers are expecting authors to drive the marketing of their books. In fact, the most successful authors draw up a marketing plan before they even start writing on their book.

Your marketing plan requires research and creative energy – skills you most likely already possess.

To get started, list your marketing plan under the following headings:

- **Book Category:** What genre/s does your book fall under? Choose books similar to yours at Amazon and see which category they are listed under.

- **Subcategories:** Which subcategories might your book fall under? For example, your category might be *Mystery, Thriller & Suspense*. At the time of writing, there are at least 40 sub-categories on Kindle including: *Noir, Amateur Sleuth, Serial Killers, Animals,* and *Outer Space*. For your book to qualify for each of these, there are certain keywords that *must* be included in your blurb.

- **Market Summary:** Provide a convincing argument that there is room for a new entrant in the market. If you can, obtain sales figures for your particular genre or subject area (e.g. 10 million romance novels were sold in the UK last year).

Is there a book similar to yours that has sold well? (e.g. my book is aimed at the same market as x by author y which sold z copies last year.) Often, you can find this information using Google, as well as authors' and publishers' websites.

- **Closest Competitors:** List your competitors (in terms of content and target audience) giving title, sub-title, publisher, publication year, and price.

- **Unique Selling Points:** Identify what is unique and different about your book.

- **Target Readers:** List the people most likely to buy your book (e.g. single women aged 18–25).

  List the types of groups, associations and clubs that might be interested in your book. Create a list of business websites, membership sites and clubs where your target readers hang out.

- **Potential Buyers:** List the types of organizations that might bulk-buy your book. This list might include: schools, colleges, universities, charities, specialist libraries and big corporates.

  List retail outlets (such as Waterstones or Barnes & Noble) and book clubs.

  List schools, colleges, universities, charities and specialist libraries that might bulk buy your books.

- **Reaching Target Readers:** Suggest ideas for bookshop promotion (e.g. a themed reading that ties in with a national anniversary or celebration).

Suggest ideas for a targeted PR campaign (e.g. a press release for local and national media). Think of a public event you could hold to tie in with your book (e.g. a quiz, a seminar, an awareness day). Suggest promotion ideas for social media (e.g. 60-second videos for YouTube, Twitter, Facebook, LinkedIn, Pinterest, Instagram, etc.).

- **PR/Awareness Raising:** Offer a free incentive to promote your book (e.g. an MP3, an online interview with the author, etc.).

    List seasonal events or anniversaries that could tie in with your book (e.g. Halloween, Mother's Day, Remembrance Day).

Brainstorm ideas for publicizing and promoting your book with a couple of friends. Write down anything and everything you can think of. Try not to censor the ideas or rule anything out. When you've finished, set your list to one side for a couple of days before going back to it. You'll be surprised at the number of great ideas you can come up with when you combine creative energy.

How to Choose The Best Book Cover

One of the favourite things I do is helping authors to choose photos or illustrations for their books. I either help them to choose images for new books that are about to be launched. Or, I help them to rebrand (and sometimes re-title) existing books that haven't been selling very well.

As research shows that 74 per cent of a reader's buying decision is based on a book cover alone, it's vital to get your book cover right.

This means paying careful attention to:

- Your book title;
- The image on the front of your book;
- Your colours;
- Your font/s;
- The blurb on the back of your book;
- The testimonials and quotes used.

In addition, your Contents page and chapter headings should be as compelling as possible as many readers look at these using the *Inside the Book* function on Amazon. I recently worked with an author who'd written a book for aspiring Forex traders with chapter headings that included: *Spreadbetting. Forex. Stop Losses.* A few simple tweaks turned these into much more compelling chapter names: How to trade without paying taxes; How to trade foreign currencies without leaving your armchair; How to protect yourself from your financial risks.

To select the right cover for the front of a book, it's essential to do a little market research, and focus on your target readership. One of the authors I've been working with recently has written a fantasy book aimed at young adults.

His designer produced 18 book covers, which the author and his team all really liked. However, when I showed these same covers to my 16-year-old son and his friends, they said things like: "these look really boring", "I don't know what it's about" and "I wouldn't read it".

To get an idea of what did appeal to them, I instead showed them a random sample of 10 fantasy books on Amazon. I asked which they liked most and what they would read. They opted for book covers that to me seemed garish, unsophisticated and even downright "cheesy" – with characters in action scenes. However, my opinion and aesthetics are totally irrelevant. Teenagers are the target readership for this book and these are the type of cover images that they clearly preferred.

"Crossover books" – books designed to appeal to both adults *and* children – usually have two entirely different covers. The *Harry Potter* books do this, for example, as do the *Northern Lights* books by Philip Pullman. Most books published globally will also have different covers, as every country will have different cultural references. The colour white may be associated with weddings and innocence in the UK, but in China it is associated with death and mourning.

For this reason, it's essential to do your market research first before you produce a book cover. Make sure you get feedback from your target audience on every aspect of your cover and what it means to them. You can contact friends and followers on social media. Or, you can do as one of my Australian clients did, which is to stand in a park and ask passers-by what they think of your book cover!

When choosing a cover image, it's also vital to consider what your long-term goals are for your book. A picture paints a thousand words. Every cover image therefore gives instant subliminal messages, based on a reader's thought associations.

Another of my non-fiction clients recently published a book to attract new clients for her pension planning business.

Here's a selection of the designs she's looked at:

1. A dinghy and a lifebelt image on the cover, to give a sense of drama and urgency.

2. A solid oak tree with rotten roots to symbolize the state of most people's finances.

3. An empty glass jar, with the label "*PENSION*" on the side, to illustrate the state of most people's finances when they hit 65.

4. A golden egg in a nest symbolizing the notion of a valuable nest egg.

5. A picture of the author on the front looking friendly and personable.

Each of these five images has its merits. However, they will each attract different types of readers. The author wishes to attract affluent middle-class professionals who are already fairly financially stable. It therefore makes less sense to have images which suggest poverty or desperation such as the dinghy, the empty pension pot or the rotten tree. Instead, the golden nest egg is much more likely to appeal, as is the picture of the author on the front. However, if she wishes to sell her business in the future, or prefers to delegate consultancy to other partners in the business, then it's probably better not to have her photo on the cover.

Gold, on the other hand, conveys a "success" message to a reader. (Think about how many best-selling books have gold lettering on the cover.) The gold nest egg image instantly conveys that the book is "special"; the gold lettering also suggests that the book is a best seller. This image is therefore much more likely to appeal to her target readership.

There are many cheap cover design services on the Internet, and lots of royalty-free vector images you can use. However, it pays to hire a professional, to do your market research, and to spend time on your book cover. I'm constantly seeing amateurish books with clip art on the front, or images that simply aren't congruent with the target readership. I also regularly see books that have been designed without "bleed" for the guillotine, which then have words or colours cropped very close to the edge.

That's why book makeovers and rebranding can work miracles for book sales. If you don't believe me, try it for yourself. Simply set up a split-test with your book. Keep your old version live on Amazon or Kindle. Then, set up a new version with a different cover and title. I can guarantee that you'll soon notice the difference.

Which Sells Best: E-Books or Paperbacks?

When I first started writing for newspapers back in 1985, we were still using Smith Corona typewriters and correction fluid. After you'd typed your story, you stuffed your sheet of paper into a small plastic canister. You then pushed this into a network of pipes to be sucked away to other floors – to the editor, to the subeditors, to the typesetters, and so on. This was the height of technology and time-saving gadgetry at the time.

When computers first started being introduced, we journalists had to retrain. Some newspaper offices had them. Others saved money and clung on to the old ways. At home, we all still had typewriters, albeit electric ones with digital screens.

Fast forward to today. Mention an Olivetti or a Remington to a teenager, and they stare back at you blankly. The only time you're likely to see a typewriter is in vintage shops or at collectors' fayres.

Change may happen so slowly you barely notice it. You can embrace it or resist it. Sometimes, it's not until you look back 10 years on that you realize it's happened. Which brings me in a roundabout way to the question: are e-books sounding the death knell for hardbacks and paperbacks? Are we witnessing the final demise of bookstores?

Joanne Harris, author of *Chocolat*, is one of many prominent authors who are acutely aware of the changes in publishing. She described to me how these changes have taken both publishers and literary agents by surprise:

"When I first signed up for Transworld, the idea of e-books was so nebulous, and there was a general feeling in the business that it would be a faddy thing that would never take off. Agents were selling e-book rights left, right, and centre; or worse, giving them for free! This happened to everybody. This wasn't very long ago – it was only 13 years ago. E-book rights were just being given for free as part of 'rights' packages. It was like audiobook rights – who really cared? It's become enormous now. It's become a whole new way of buying and perceiving books. It will get bigger and bigger, I think."

American author, Sharon Lechter, is an astute businesswoman, as well as co-author of the best seller, *Rich Dad, Poor Dad*. She predicts further sweeping changes in the years to come:

"The world of publishing has changed dramatically in the past 10 years. And I follow that by saying the world of publishing has changed in the past two years. The world of publishing will change dramatically in the next year: because of the presence of online ordering ability and Amazon being a dot-com; because of the number of bookstores that are going out of business; and because of the rising popularity of e-books. All of those dynamics impact how to become a successful author and have multiple sales. You need to make sure your book is available in as many formats as possible ..."

These predictions are backed up by sales figures from the world's top authors. There's no denying the popularity and rise of e-books.

Novelist, Jeffrey Archer, whose books have sold over 270 million copies, has seen a massive change in the way readers are buying his books and the way in which his writing is promoted:

"Five years ago, I'd say 5 per cent of my sales were on e-books;

it's now 50 per cent ... They don't bother to send me to New York now. They say, 'Put a blog out, put a tweet out, Jeffrey. Let everybody know it's coming,' and my fans read the blogs or the tweets or Facebook, so they know it's coming. If I go to San Francisco, 150 or 200 people come out for a signing session. It's not worth it!"

Anne Rice, author of *Interview with the Vampire*, told me that she's also noticed the dramatic changes in sales of her books: "It's changing rapidly. On my last novel, the last I heard, they were 50 per cent. For every 100 hardcovers, they were selling maybe 50 e-books. So the total for e-books was half of the final total for hardcovers. So that's amazing, because it was not that way in the past, but e-books are gaining popularity every week ... All the time, you see more and more people recommending e-books. In the beginning, it was a minority. Now they're all admitting that they're going to e-books for various reasons."

There are wider implications for authors too – such as less face-to-face contact with readers when it comes to book launches. Instead, writers are more likely to market and promote a book via social media.

Anne Rice says she's getting the same demand as usual to go on tour. However, the problem is the bookstores aren't there any more. "I'm getting a lot of requests to come sign in this place or that place, a lot of requests to meet people individually in an autograph line. I think that will continue but the problem is, the bookstores where we used to go over the years – to have these wonderful big signings – they don't exist any more. They're dying out. They're closing. They're gone!" she explains.

Bernard Cornwell, author of the *Sharpe* series, estimates that around 60 per cent of his novels are being sold as e-books in the American market. He confesses reading on an iPad, and his wife Judy on a Kindle.

"I don't know whether it's good or bad. A fish doesn't complain about the sea it swims in. I don't know where it's going. One part of me thinks I'm awfully glad that I had my career before e-books came in. But another part of me thinks you probably sell more e-books at a slightly lower price than you do of physical books."

However, he notes a darker side of digital publishing: "My big worry is when somebody manages to break the code. Already, if you go online – and you'll find this with every author you're interviewing – there must be 20 or 30 sites that are offering my books at a dollar or one pound each. What they've done is, some guy has sat there and scanned the whole book and they're selling a PDF edition. They're all over the damn place!

"They try to take them down if they can. I know that all the publishers get together and hire someone, or a company, that scours the Internet to find these people. I'm not too worried about the PDF, because who wants to read a whole book in a PDF version? It's going to be really a pretty gruesome experience. But eventually someone's going to crack the code and the books will be out there. Look what happened to the music industry. File sharing could kill us, but I don't know enough about it to talk about the technicalities."

Personally, I love to have a glossy book that I can flick through. I've always enjoyed browsing in bookstores. Yet I confess that I also like the 24/7 accessibility of e-books, the speed, the instant access, the lack of clutter in my home.

I'd hate to think we are witnessing the demise of paperbacks and bookstores. But I wonder if I am contributing to it, and in 10 years time if teenagers will stare back blankly when you mention the words "paperback" or "hardback".

How to Get a Celebrity Endorsement For Your Book

Getting a celebrity endorsement for your book is one of the easiest ways to promote it. Readers are much more likely to listen to a well-known expert or media personality saying they can't put your book down. Not only this, but a little "celebrity" magic tends to rub off on you.

Many authors are reluctant to approach celebrities for testimonials. Don't make the same mistake! I'm not saying that you should write to every celebrity or expert you can think of willy-nilly. However, if there is a tie-in with your book, however tenuous, then go for it.

Celebrities have egos the same as everyone else. Some actors and actresses even crave the limelight while they are "resting" between TV productions or movie contracts. And if your book is getting publicity and media attention, this is also going to benefit them.

You may have to approach 100, even 200, celebrities. But you only need *one* to make a massive difference to your book sales. Does it really matter if 199 tell you to get lost, if you get the one testimonial you're after? What do you stand to lose? Hurt pride and the time it took to write the message or make the phone call!

It's never been easier to access celebrities via the Internet. Not only can you use search engines like Google to track them down; many of them also have Facebook and Twitter accounts. Make it easy for them by writing five of your own testimonials. When you contact them, point out that you appreciate they might be stretched for time so they can choose one of your templates if they wish. Anything that saves them time or having to wade through loads of material will persuade them of your professionalism.

If conventional celebrities feel too daunting, then think about people with professional credentials relating to your book. These might be people such as bank managers, doctors, police officers, teachers or life coaches. While they might not be on TV, their professional titles have an "expert" or "authority" status that can be just as powerful.

If you're feeling daunted, then focus on the positive benefits for yourself and your book. Quotes will boost your book sales and credibility. And think how great you'll feel when you see those endorsements printed on your book cover.

How Do I Get My Book into Airport Stores?

Many authors love the idea of their book being in airport stores while a captive audience is milling around, with time on their hands and money to spend. Even a short book promotion campaign has a potential audience of over a billion airline passengers – so it's well worth doing.

If this is your big dream, then you need to know that Hudson News (based in New Jersey) and The Paradies Shops (a family-run business in Georgia) are the largest players in global airport sales.

There's a lot of competition with pitching books to their headquarters, so this is something that requires a lot of skill and isn't really for amateurs. First, you need a first-class cover, with "pick me up" factor. Second, you need a best-selling title.

Finally, you need a compelling and attention-grabbing blurb.

Ideally, you need feedback from a publishing professional that your book has all these traits. Otherwise, you may not – don't make the mistake of asking well-intentioned friends and family for advice.

A "really good" book is not enough here: you need to have an exceptional book with wow factor! You're likely to get one bite at the cherry, so don't blow your chances by going in with a weak pitch. It also helps to offer a special "cooperative rate". In other words, you have to offer a reduction on the first order over and above the regular discount that's usually offered to retailers.

However, beware – especially if you're a self-publisher – that return rates range between 60 and 70 per cent. So "sale or return" can mean that you end up with a heap of unsold books and a fresh challenge of how you're going to sell them. That is, unless your book really takes off, in which case reorders will rapidly start to happen.

Next time you're an airline passenger, take a look at the books currently available in the stores. Read the airplane magazines during your flight. Make a mental note of the type of articles that are included. Ask yourself whether your book might be a good fit for this publication. But again, you'll need a strong pitch. This is a highly competitive market, so you need to be certain that everything about your book is first class.

If you're successful securing space inside an airport bookstore, then you have a very short time-span to generate sales. Tell everyone you know about it. Take a photo of your book in one of the stores and post it on all your social media. Create some hype and encourage your clients and subscribers to tell others. Start a "spot my book" competition for travellers and ask them to take photos. Remember that excitement is highly contagious!

Airlines provide a captive audience, seeking entertainment and distraction, every single day of the week. It's well worth investing time and energy to make this happen for your book.

Should You Print More Copies of Your Self-Published Book or Is This Madness?

Self-published authors frequently ask me: "Should I pay for another print run of my book?" They're usually confused by cleverly-written marketing blurb that's trying to lure them into spending yet more money.

Here's the standard scenario. You've already handed over your hard-earned cash to a self-publishing or printing company and your book has barely been on sale for a week.

Then, wham! You're sent a tantalizing "special offer" suggesting that they print you an extra 3,000 copies for the greatly reduced price of £6,000. They've "discounted" this price down from an astronomical sum like £15,000 to make it sound super-enticing.

Your "personal invitation" describes the plight of disappointed readers hunting high and low for your book in high-street shops, but having to go away empty-handed. They cleverly argue that an extra print run will ensure a copy of your book in every bookstore in the United States or Australia or New Zealand or Japan – or wherever it is that might take your fancy. They point out that this "discount" will improve your profit margins as the price of bulk printing is much lower. They might even call it something fancy like "offset printing" or "an offset print run".

Very thoughtful and altruistic of them, I must say, to put so much time and effort into thinking about your profit margins rather than theirs! Especially when the price of all this is the equivalent of a week in a five-star hotel.

OK, let's get serious for a moment. Because I'm about to save you money, time, and possibly even your sanity. I strongly recommend that you do *not* get out your credit card or pay another dime until you have sold at least 1,000 copies of your book *minimum*.

Here's why:

1. Only one in seven books is bought in bookshops. Contrary to what these "Smart Alec" copywriters may be arguing, most people go online if they want to buy a book. You need to establish your market online *first*, before you plunge into the offline market. Why saturate a market with books that are likely to gather dust on the shelves or end up in remainder bins?

2. Passionate and enthusiastic buyers aren't that bothered about the price of a book. If people don't buy, it'll be because your book cover's not attractive enough. It'll be because your blurb's not compelling enough. Or maybe your topic doesn't interest them. Seriously. Think about your own behaviour when you spot a book you feel excited about and passionately want. Are you going to change your mind just because it's £3 more than you want it to be? I don't think so. Readers are much more influenced by emotional factors like perceived value – and "value" isn't always quantified in pounds and pence. It's how important something feels in a particular moment.

3. You need a proper marketing plan to tackle any market, let alone the USA, Australia, New Zealand or any other territory. If you don't have one, then you're not really serious about the success of your book. If you don't already

have proper mechanisms in place for driving customers to your website to buy your books, what makes you think they are going to find your book in overfilled bookshops?

4. You need to do some comprehensive research before the launch of any product – and yes, unromantic as it might seem, a book qualifies as a "product". Surely you'd want to see a proven demand before blasting the market with thousands of shiny new paperbacks?

The only exception to this is if you're already 110 per cent certain that you have a strong marketing and publicity strategy in place and that every one of your books is going to be sold. Unless you're already an experienced self-publisher with many book sales under your belt, it's unlikely you can be this certain.

Don't get me wrong. I absolutely want you to have confidence in your book. I absolutely want you to have faith that your books will sell. But that confidence and faith needs to be backed up with research and a powerful marketing plan. Leaping in without this is just madness!

Why It Pays to Grow a List of Fans on Social Media

Many authors are so focused on writing their books they neglect the bigger picture. But if you genuinely want to attract a publisher or an agent, you need to go the extra mile to grab their attention.

Here's a recent question from one of my subscribers that I'd like to share … and my answer:

How would you interpret an agent who writes three paragraphs gushing about how much she enjoyed the writer making so much effort to get her attention and then summing it up with, "However, the book is not for us." Do you think it's time to give up?

My reply in brief:

This means exactly what it says on the tin. They love the book, but it's not for them. Loosely translated, they can see you're a great writer, but they don't feel the passion and excitement that's essential to represent a book.

No, you definitely should not give up. Agents wouldn't give you the time of day if they didn't think you had talent. The current publishing environment is incredibly tough. For this reason, your pitch needs a big dose of "oomph!" or uniqueness to stand out.

I strongly recommend building yourself a "platform" or "list" of fans for your writing. This can be done via social media such as Facebook, Twitter or LinkedIn. Some publishers won't even look at authors who have less than 5,000 friends on Facebook. So building up your list of followers can sometimes sway the case in your favour.

Here's a different letter from one of my other subscribers which reflects the difference this can make:

My daughter is on the cusp of a book deal. She has an agent after following your advice in your "Get an Agent" course. We found your advice invaluable, especially the advice about creating social networking interest.

Her agent told her that her web presence and web profile was the main factor in taking her on – something we would not have known about had we not attended your workshop.

One word of advice about this. When you grow a list on social media, it's essential to be strategic about it. There's no point in randomly friending anyone and everyone. Instead, identify authors who have written books similar to yours, or groups where readers are interested in your topic. These are the people you want to target as they are most likely to be interested in you. (You've probably heard the phrase, "birds of a feather stick together"?)

At a time when publishers are being sent hundreds of manuscripts each week, you need strategies to make yourself and your book stand out from all the others. If you can persuade them that you already have a following *before* your book is even published, they will see you are highly motivated, driven and therefore marketable.

All this can only reflect well on you … and help you land the book deal you deserve.

How To Turn Your Book into an Amazon Best Seller

If you've written a book or if you want to get your message out to the world, there has never been an easier time to become a best-selling author. The Internet has provided writers with an unprecedented opportunity to spread their message and reach more readers at a faster rate than ever before.

So let me take you step by step through the process of how to turn your book into a best seller and gain more readers.

Your number one priority is to give away something of value to your potential readers. That might sound back to font – but trust me, it isn't. You might give away valuable content such as: a "how-to" article; a free e-book or report; an e-zine; a teleseminar; or an MP3.

If you're pressed for time, team up with other experts who can provide this free content. So if your book is about dog breeding, contact other pet experts. Or if your book is about gardening, contact high-profile gardening experts (preferably those with a large database or "list" of clients).

Tell them you're offering the chance to promote their business if they'd like to offer something for free in return. It's a win-win situation: they provide you with a freebie, you promote their website to your readers.

When you put a value on these free bonuses, it can run into thousands of dollars. This makes a $9.99 book phenomenal value – in fact, readers will sometimes buy a book just to get their hands on the bonuses.

On the day your book is launched, ask all the experts who gave free bonuses to help promote it. They can do this via their own mailing lists, as well as social media such as Facebook and Twitter. They may even want to bulk-buy your book at discount to sell to their own clients. If everyone promotes your book on the same day, you can very quickly push your book onto the best seller list for your particular niche on Amazon.

Even if it only hovers there for three minutes, that's all it takes. The kudos of having a best-selling book lasts a lifetime. It will open doors for you when you're looking for speaking engagements or business partnerships. It makes you stand out when you send out press releases to journalists. And, if you become a No1 best-selling author, it positions you alongside the other leaders in your field.

How To Get Your Book Serialized in Newspapers and Glossy Magazines

Most authors find the idea of pitching or promoting their book to newspapers, magazines, radio and television daunting. However, you presumably wrote (or are writing) your book because you feel you have something worthwhile to say. So it's worth making sure as many readers get to hear about it as possible.

One of the biggest mistakes authors (and indeed, some PR consultants) make, is to assume that your press release should be sent out mainly to book reviewers. To my mind, this is a massive error. A book review tends to have postage-stamp-sized coverage, with a teeny image of your book cover if you're lucky. What's more, someone has to actually read your 70,000 plus words before this can happen. Yes, book reviews are influential in selling books. But organising them is time-consuming and unreliable.

If you send your press release to a specific science editor, features writer, reporter or broadcaster instead, you power up your PR campaign considerably. *Saga Magazine*, for example, secured first serialization rights for my book *Celebrity Authors' Secrets*. This spanned six pages and included four photographs, plus an image of my book jacket, as well as a double-page illustration. There was also a listing and a photo on the Contents page, as well as a headline on the front cover. If I paid for similar coverage in advertising to their 1.8 million readers, the cost would have run into tens of thousands.

Journalists like stories that are:

- topical (an event or activity that's linked to a trending news topic);
- inspirational (ordinary people doing extraordinary things);
- educational (improves health, wealth or relationships);
- unexpected (eat more chocolate, get slim);
- controversial statements (women are worse bosses);
- "then-and-now" contrasts (you were overweight/broke/depressed etc. and now you're the opposite);
- a big promise (lose wrinkles in seven days with facial yoga).

Remember that most journalists won't have time to read your book. So bullet-point the necessary facts. Or write your press release about you and your inspiration, or anything else that is interesting and relevant. Another approach is to create an event or photo opportunity for them to attend.

Here are some quick and easy guidelines for structuring your press release:

- Headline – start with something that's likely to grab attention.
- Paragraph 1 – summarize your "story" giving key information.
- Paragraph 2/3 – flesh out your story – who, why, what, where and when.

- Paragraph 4 – include a quote from you or someone relevant.

- Paragraph 5 – include any extra information such as a photo opportunity.

- Final Paragraph – include the all-important sentence: *"For a review copy, permission to use printed extracts, or to arrange an interview, contact xyz."*

- Contact Details: phone, Skype and email.

- If the story is for immediate release, say so. If it's embargoed until a certain date, this gives journalists time to prepare ahead.

Take time to tailor your press release for different publications. Suppose, for example, you've written a dieting book. Your press release for health magazines might look at psychological and physical topics. For national newspapers, you might include more statistical evidence. For regional media, you might mention a "local angle".

Like all things, it takes a while to master new skills. But eventually, you'll learn to do this on "autopilot" and may even start to enjoy it. It will also leverage your time considerably. Compare the potential return on investment for an hour spent writing your press release with that of an hour spent giving a reading in a local library or bookshop. To my mind, it's a no-brainer to send out your press release to as many journalists as you can to get maximum coverage.

And if several publications want serialization rights for your book? Then, you need to weigh up what your long-term goals are and whether their target readership is the same as yours.

Also, think about which media logo you'd most like to have on your website and branding, and which one is most likely to appeal to your target readers. This is rather a nice problem for any author to have!

Why Bother with Journalists? It Sounds Like Too Much Effort!

Many authors wrongly assume that their book isn't important enough, or that only celebrities and famous writers get interviewed by the media. This just isn't true. Radio stations (particularly local radio stations) have many hours of airtime to fill each day. Similarly, many print publications are also looking for inspiring, topical, or controversial human interest stories to entertain their readers.

You may be thinking: "It sounds like a lot of hard work. I don't know if I can be bothered." But here's why it matters: many newspapers and magazines have audiences that run into millions. For example, *The Huffington Post*, for which I am a blogger, has over 30 million readers globally. Many other newspapers, magazines and radio stations have similar-sized audiences. Even if only 10% read about your book, that's still a massive audience that you're reaching.

When you're interviewed or reviewed, this phenomenal coverage costs nothing, zilch, other than your time and energy. Yet, in return you can build a massive following for your book even *before* it's launched. So it makes sense – enormous sense – to spend time mastering this.

When authors do approach the media, a common mistake I see is that the press release ends up sounding like a pitch-a-thon for the book. Most journalists don't have time to read books. They may not even be interested in your book, period. But what they *are* interested in is you, the story of what inspired you to write your book, or the fact that you're an expert who can comment on a similar topic that's in the news. In other words, your book is not necessarily the reason *why* you will get media coverage. It does however give you a *big reason* to attract the media's attention.

Another common mistake is to write the *same* press release for multiple publications. To give a real-life example from a PR campaign for one of my books, many of *Saga Magazine*'s readers are aged over 50 and interested in becoming authors – so a press release about publishing secrets worked fine for them. However, when approaching women's magazines or celebrity magazines, my press release was angled towards more personal (rather than professional) aspects of famous authors' lives. So I looked at interesting "trivia" about their day-to-day lives and the sacrifices they have to make to write their books. This is much more in keeping with the gossipy nature of these magazines and what their audiences like to read.

All authors can use this strategy to get publicity for books. It's remarkably simple and you can do it in less than a day. It's just a matter of writing a one-page press release and identifying where to send it. I recently helped a very shy and retiring author, who'd never had much success with the media, to write her own press release. Then, I gave her a script for what to say to news editors and features writers. Within a couple of hours, she'd secured a feature in *The Observer* and six months of articles in *The Nursing Times*.

If you've never done this before, try your hand at it this weekend. Just see what you can achieve.

How to Prepare for a Radio or Television Interview

Getting your book publicized on radio or television is exciting. It gives you instant "celebrity" status and a larger audience than you would have in a book store or library. So it goes without saying that media interviews are worth agreeing to.

While many authors may feel a bit star-struck (or terrified!) it's essential to do some preparation before you go live on air.

List all the questions that journalists are most likely to ask you, then write down your answers. Also write down "tricky" questions that you'd perhaps rather they didn't ask. Remember that it's OK to say things like "I don't feel qualified to answer that right now" or "I'm not really the right person for you to ask". This sounds much better than "no comment".

Journalists love interviewees who use sound bites. You'll notice that TV and radio often use 30-second clips taken from lengthier interviews. Newspapers and magazines also use them as headlines or subtitles.

If you master the art of sound bites, you'll find that journalists come back to you again and again. The aim is to condense a complex idea into just one or two sentences, with a bit of zing!

Here are some handy tips to help you prepare for a memorable interview:

1. Keep it brief.

Condense your ideas to one to two sentences maximum.

2. Use metaphors.

I attended a press conference around 25 years ago at Sizewell B nuclear reactor in Suffolk while I was working as a newsreader and journalist. There was a scare about radioactivity at the time. The press officer told the assembled journalists that: "The amount of uranium used at the reactor each year is less than the size of a brazil nut." I understood very little about the science of nuclear power, but it sounded small and insignificant and I still remember it to this day.

See if you can find metaphors or comparisons that draw on the subjects in your book.

3. Voice a strong opinion.

Many people are scared to give their opinions for fear others will disagree. The media prefer people with strong opinions, rather than people who sit on the fence. If you feel passionately about something, stand up for your beliefs.

4. Use repetition of words or phrases.

Repeating one or two words can give a rhythmic and memorable momentum to a sentence, while making your point. For example, Warren Buffett, on investing: "Be fearful when others are greedy and greedy when others are fearful." Do be wary of overdoing this technique though. Once or twice is fine. More than this is too much.

5. Use surprising statistics or figures.

Research figures around your subject, especially surprises that no one else is likely to know.

For example: *2.5 million old copies of Mills & Boon books were used to build the M6 motorway. On some stretches of UK motorway, 4,500 pulped books have been used for every mile of tarmac.*

Sound bites are usually attention-grabbing and therefore help to attract readers, listeners and viewers. Also, journalists and newsreaders frequently have to cut stories at the last minute to make room for breaking news. They therefore use the most memorable phrases to summarize the story or grab readers' attention.

6. Call to action.

Authors sometimes complain to me that they've had lots of radio or newspaper interviews, but nothing tangible has resulted from them. This is why it's essential to have a call to action for anyone who listens to or reads your interview.

Examples of a call to action might be: "Buy my book on Amazon" or "Sign up to my free newsletter" or "I'm offering the first 30 listeners who contact me a free consultation". This ensures that you get something back from your interviews. Otherwise you run the risk of spending time being interviewed by journalists without a return on your time.

Finally, enjoy the experience. You worked hard on your book and you deserve your success. Enjoy your moment in the spotlight!

How To Fill A Room And Market Your Event in 7 Easy Steps

Authors sometimes invite me to seminars, workshops or conferences they've organized to tie in with their books ... then a couple of months down the line I discover that the event's been cancelled as they haven't managed to sell enough tickets.

They start out passionate and excited, with a fantastic idea. But they end up disheartened feeling that "it's too difficult" and "people just aren't interested".

First of all, let me say that I always have jitters in the lead-up to my own events, wondering whether or not I will fill a room. This is normal and to be expected. However, what is important is to follow a proven step-by-step plan to ensure your event is a success.

When I first started out, I had zero experience of holding big events for 400 plus people. But what I did have was determination to succeed and, with three small children to provide for, failure simply wasn't an option.

My game plan therefore was to learn "the formula" for filling an event and to stick to it. As a result, every event I've held over the past four years has exceeded expectations – I've had to upgrade venues at the last minute, and even move back the stage to make room for more seats!

So here are my top tips for marketing your event and getting the proverbial "bums on seats":

1. Tickets

Consider carefully how you will fill your room. One method is to give away free tickets which, in my experience, means that only around 30–40 per cent of people with tickets will show up. The advantage of this method is that attracts a bigger number of attendees much, much faster. You can also build a sizeable list of prospects who you can sell to at a later date. The downside is that they may not be very committed.

The other strategy is to sell tickets – which is much harder to do. But what it does mean is that you will have a much more committed audience. Anything from 70–90 per cent will turn up. Not only this, but if you decide to sell products or services to them, then they will be much more inclined to buy.

2. Four-Month Lead-In

Give yourself sufficient time to plan your event. A copywriter will typically take two weeks to write your sales letter. A web designer will take around the same length of time to put up your website. That's after you've waited for speakers to send back their photos, bios and contracts. You need to allow yourself sufficient time to write and prepare your marketing materials and PR in advance. Give yourself a buffer period so that if something doesn't go as planned, you still have plenty of time to set things right.

3. Know Your Target Audience

What is it that your target audience most wants to know? What is it they ardently desire? What is it that they fear? Tailor your event so that it meets all their needs and becomes a "no-brainer" for them to attend. It's vital that you understand your audience before you do anything else. Try to put yourself in their minds and think as they think. If they don't attend or don't come along, why not? What is most likely to hold them back? Then address these issues.

4. Partnerships

Partnerships (or joint ventures) are vital to filling a room. Before approaching someone about a partnership, consider what's in it for them? Are you going to offer them a reciprocal mail-out? Are you going to give them a commission? Will you let them speak at your event? What will you offer them that's of value in return? It has to be a win-win situation for them to want to be involved. Ensure also that your partners are in the same niche as you. If not, you may find yourself sending out a promotional email to a list of 100,000 and getting zero response in return. (Take it from someone who has made this mistake!)

5. Affiliates

Affiliate programmes are easier to set up than you think. For several years, I avoided doing this because it sounded too complicated. When I first set one up, I really started to see sales rolling in. Offer as high a percentage commission as you can. Typically, I offer 100 per cent commission, but 50 per cent is also a good incentive. The profits can always come from sales of higher-priced services on the day of your event. The people who attend are also much more likely to be your target audience, rather than what are commonly known as "tyre kickers".

6. Free Bonuses

Make sure that you offer valuable free gifts and bonuses to draw people in. It's best if these are downloadable freebies such as MP3s or e-books. Often the bonuses I give out are worth hundreds or even thousands of pounds, and worth 20 times more than the ticket value. Sometimes, I find people attend purely on the basis of the bonuses because they can see the tremendous value that's being offered!

7. Social Media

Use social media such as Facebook, Twitter and YouTube to promote your event. Invite friends and acquaintances along. Share the links with as many people as possible and create a buzz around your event. You can even interview some of the speakers beforehand to build up hype in advance. Social media costs nothing and can reach an audience of thousands. Traditional advertising, in contrast, can be expensive and also reaches a much smaller audience. Try to leverage your time and money as much as possible to get the maximum "bang for your buck".

Finally, stayed connected with your heart source and with passion. People are often cynical of a "salesy" approach. However, they can feel the difference with someone sincere who loves what they do and genuinely wants to help others.

Enjoy your event. There's little more satisfying than seeing a room filled with people and knowing that your energy and enthusiasm helped to draw them there!

Would You Let TV Cameras into Your Home?

When I was first asked if I'd like to take part in a new BBC television series about family life, I imagined a brief interview and a couple of shots of my young daughters playing Monopoly with their teenage brother. "Why not?" I thought.

But when the TV producer called me, it turned out they wanted to rig cameras in our home for several weeks and have a crew here for "special occasions".

"Special occasions, such as?" I ventured.

Oh, just the usual run-of-the-mill stuff: "Birthdays, family gatherings ..."

By a stroke of sheer genius, we'd also be given our own handheld cameras to do "selfies" and put us "in control". Nothing to worry about then.

"Let me discuss it with my partner," I said, to buy myself a bit of time. I think I may have been hyperventilating slightly by this point.

Once I'd calmed down a little, I thought it would be a bit of lark to run the idea past my partner with my "serious" face on. Bad move. It's the closest I've ever seen him to heart failure. The thought of my eight-year-old holding a "selfie" camera at the breakfast table was too much.

"Just let me know when I can move back in," he said, ashen-faced. My mother had a few choice words to say too, as did many of my friends and clients. The sense of fear, dread and outright horror was palpable. Interestingly, there were also those who just said: "YES! Go for it!"

As a book publicist and marketing strategist, working with authors on press campaigns and book launches, this whole experience raised a lot of interesting questions for me. How much publicity is "good" publicity? What is "bad" publicity? Is there too high a price for marketing a book?

A media campaign is a vital part of launching and promoting many new books. A slot on national TV can give you exposure to millions of potential readers who've never heard of you before. You only have to look at an Amazon sales graph to see the impact on book orders. There are often sharp spikes on the days when radio shows are broadcast or magazines are put on the news stands.

Most authors have different responses to the idea of a media campaign. Many don't believe they're "famous" enough to be in the media. Others fear they'll be portrayed in a bad light or that their words will be twisted. Some embrace the idea with enthusiasm, keen for celebrity status.

So how can you take advantage of the opportunities that the media offers – assuming you want to take them – while at the same time protecting your reputation and privacy?

Here are some brief guidelines to give you confidence for any interview:

- Research the publication, programme, or journalist before you agree to speak to them. Are they serious, fun, silly, gossipy, bitchy? How they treat other interviewees is a good indication of how they'll treat you.
- Make a list of questions they're likely to ask based on the 5 Ws: who, why, what, where, when.

- Prepare and rehearse your answers.

- Make a list of awkward questions and then prepare carefully considered replies. You may never need this, but preparation is the key to staying calm. It's better to give an answer you've spent time thinking about than to be caught off guard.

- It's OK to say: "That's a great question. But that's not really my area of expertise." This approach makes you sound confident and assertive, whereas dodging the question or being evasive, sounds suspicious.

- Use the recording app on your smartphone or buy a Dictaphone to record the interview. Tell the journalist politely but firmly that you're keeping this for your own records. Most journalists are super-careful with any interviewee who has a duplicate recording!

- Have a clear "call to action" for your readers or listeners such as "friend me on Facebook" or "sign up for my updates on Twitter". This ensures that your interview has clear and tangible results.

- If you're clever, you can use your interview to build your list of potential customers. So offer an ethical bribe (such as a free ticket to an event or an e-book) to encourage people to sign up to your newsletter or email list.

As for having cameras rigged in your home, that's a decision only you can make. Some authors want privacy; others want celebrity. My decision: I prefer eating my cornflakes in peace. Besides, I'm not sure my partner's heart can take many more surprises. Beta blockers, anyone?!

Do You Have What It Takes to Be a Millionaire Author?

We often hear the romantic story of J. K. Rowling penning her first *Harry Potter* novel in her local coffee shop, her baby daughter sleeping alongside her. The atmosphere sounds friendly and familiar. It feels achievable – even effortless – to write your own book.

But this is a far cry from the reality of most millionaire authors' lives. I'm fortunate to have worked with many of the world's greatest authors ... and it's definitely not a life for the faint-hearted. Yes, they make it look easy. They glide like swans across the surface of a crystal lake – but under the water, their feet are often paddling like crazy.

Barbara Taylor Bradford, author of *A Woman of Substance*, has written 28 novels and sold over 89 million copies. Yet she'll often rise at 4.30 a.m. or 5 a.m. when she's writing a book and will carry on working until 4 p.m.: "I don't accept lunch invitations unless it is a business thing and I have to, or it is somebody's celebration, someone's birthday, because I think it kills the day for me," she explains.

Even with 270 million copies sold, Jeffrey Archer also rises at 5.30 a.m. – when most ordinary mortals are still in bed – and writes on and off until 8 p.m.: "It's sheer hard work, sheer discipline," he admits. "To young people who say, 'I've written a book,' I say, 'I doubt it; you've probably written a first draft!' My books have had 13 or 14 drafts, every one of them handwritten. So, it's hard work and it's a marathon every time. You've got to accept that it's a marathon, and if you're not willing to, well ..."

Not only are the hours long, but millionaire authors also set themselves formidable word counts and daily writing targets. Anne Rice, author of *Interview with the Vampire*, often writes 15 to 20 pages per day: "I've written whole books totally at night! Even recently, I wrote them at night to get away from all distractions, but I can't do it any more. I get very sick from that kind of upset schedule, and I guess my body is just too old to do it," she confesses.

While many first-time authors take over a year to write their books, Alexander McCall Smith, bestselling author of *The No. 1 Ladies' Detective Agency*, produces three or four books per year. He's written over 100 books now, but still wishes he could write even more: "I've actually genuinely stopped counting. I know that that sounds affected, but I really have. So I don't know how many I've written," he says.

It doesn't seem to matter which genre best-selling authors are writing in. When they're at the top of their game, they do whatever it takes to stay on top. Motivational guru Brian Tracy, best-selling author of *Eat That Frog*, has written over 60 business books, yet still aims to write a new book every 90 days: "I'm producing eight this year: six of which are already in the market; the other two will be in the market this fall. My goal was to produce a book every 90 days, and I've done that now consistently for 12 or 13 years," he explains.

I have mentioned just a few aspects of the process of writing a book. The millionaire authors I've worked with apply the same gargantuan effort to: their book launches; to marketing; to promotion; to speaking; to media appearances; to touring.

Over 70 US authors have sold over a million copies of their book since Nielsen BookScan started keeping records in 1986.

The personal sacrifices, the extremes of preparation, and the daily regime of pushing oneself to the limits are similar to those required of an Olympian athlete.

This isn't just about going the proverbial "extra mile" for your profession. This isn't even about going an extra 100 miles. It goes beyond discipline, beyond work ethic, beyond enthusiasm. It's obsession. It's addiction. It's living and breathing your book, day in, day out. It's not about writing being a part of your life, but writing *being* your life.

Many people think it's down to chance which books sell millions and which don't. Experience tells me otherwise. Too many authors dash off books, plonk them on Amazon, then wonder when they don't sell. Or they get a handful of rejections from publishers and moan about how "difficult" it is to sell books these days.

The fact is there's a reason why some authors sell millions of books and others struggle to sell even 100 copies. This isn't down to luck or chance. The question is: are you willing to make this your obsession?

How to Make More Money from Your Book

I went for lunch with a best-selling author this week. I took him to Malmaison in Oxford (a former prison, but now a very swish 5-star establishment). The author has sold over 50,000 books and is one of the leading experts in his field. He's published 3 books with a major publisher. He's at the pinnacle of his literary career. So he should be rolling in it. Right?

But you know what? In his own words, he's made "chicken feed" from his books and he's still stuck in a job he'd rather not be in. His work leaves little or no time for his true passion, writing.

"I'm coming up to retirement," he said. "But I've yet to make any real money from my books."

Fifty thousand books: that's 50,000 readers! But like so many authors, he has *no* idea who these readers are! He has no names or addresses, and no means of contacting them. So the power rests in the hands of his publisher who dictates what his publishing advance and royalties will be – which is not a lot.

So here's the advice I gave this author: start collecting names and addresses and building a list of your readers. Start a free newsletter for them. Put an opt-in box on your website to collect names and addresses. If possible, automate the newsletter. Use a service such as getresponse.com or aweber.com, so that you can send out emails to your subscribers at the touch of a button.

I know I keep banging on about this to my clients, but having your own database or list of readers is an absolute *must* if you're ever going to make money as an author. The first sale of a book is always going to be the hardest. The second – to a converted "fan" – is so much easier.

Millionaire authors know that "the money is in the list". They never waste an opportunity to promote themselves or build their relationship with their readers by writing blogs, newsletters or e-zines. This means they collect names and addresses when they give talks or lectures. When they give radio or TV interviews, they use it as an excuse to mention their websites. They use the spare pages at the back of their books to advertise their e-zines.

The big money is rarely in book sales. It's in higher-priced products and services that are linked to the book. Get to know who your readers are. Try to understand them and build a relationship with them.

The majority of authors don't know who their readers are … don't make the same mistake.

How to Host a Book Launch that Doesn't Suck

The most memorable literary event I've ever attended was held at an art gallery in London. I'd been a judge for some writers' awards. It was a black-tie event so everyone was dressed up to the nines.

Halfway through the evening, the doors were sealed, security guards appeared and a "surprise guest" was announced. Salman Rushdie walked in looking very dapper, gave a speech, mingled, and promptly disappeared again.

It was in the early 1990s, just after he had gone into hiding. But I still remember it like it was yesterday. I can still see those canapés dusted with gold icing, the artistic bowls they were served in, and the strategically placed minimalist sculptures. We were mesmerized even before Salman entered the room. When he did, we were blown away. The thought and planning that went into that event were phenomenal.

Equally, I've known of some pretty dire events. At the worst end of the scale, a multimillionaire business author hired a mansion in an exclusive part of London and sold tickets, promoting it as an opportunity to mix with high-net-worth entrepreneurs. He had a large cake made, with the cover of his book on it, and set up a "mini-bar" and a sound system.

What happened next by all accounts was a cross between a rugby scrum and a school disco. More people showed up than expected, and jostled with each other for space. Wine had to be served from boxes in white plastic cups. The neighbours complained about the goings-on next door, and the landlord was called. No permission had been given to hold an event of this scale on the premises, so everyone was asked to leave. Not quite the impression you would want to give, unless perhaps you are one of the Gallagher brothers.

Generally though, book launches tend to follow a pretty standard format whether they're held in bookshops, libraries or galleries. A glass of Merlot awaits you when you roll up. You stand around mingling with the great and the good for an hour. The author makes a speech about their book, gives a short reading, and thanks everyone who has helped them. A request is made for you to buy the book if you haven't already. Half an hour later, it's time to go home. You've enjoyed yourself, but there's very little to distinguish one event from another.

So the question is: how can you host a memorable book launch that really stands out, regardless of your budget? Any author can do this if you use the same creativity that went into writing your book in the first place:

1. Find a venue that complements your book

A bookshop or library is a safe, but conventional, option. If you're looking for something more prestigious, then pick an upmarket venue like a museum or a country house. If it's the height of summer, then consider a BBQ in a park, beach or garden. If you're a speaker, then why not tie in your book launch with a talk you're giving? If you're a children's author, can you hold the event in a school, a cinema or a zoo? If you have the resources, how about a boat or a castle? One of my clients wrote her book on her laptop while sitting in Costa's, so it was natural for her to host a signing there. You don't have to spend a fortune to make an impact.

2. Set the mood for the event

How can you set the mood from the moment your guests walk in? Do you want candlelight, daylight, or fluorescent lighting? Will your guests drink from plastic cups, glass goblets or champagne flutes? Will you offer them Beaujolais or bubbly? Will they have cheese on cocktail sticks, or something more exotic? Will they be served on paper plates or silver platters? Will the room be decorated in bunting or photographs that tie in with your book? Roller banners, with your business logo or your book cover, are a very cost-effective way to make an impression.

3. What will your photos look like?

Imagine a photograph of yourself signing a book at your launch. Would you prefer the event to have a serious or a fun feel? Would you like attendees to wear dress suits or jeans? Should it be upmarket or informal? Is this a no-children affair or a family event? How about a theme where people wear fancy dress? If you've written a novel set in the 1920s, could you play jazz, serve mint julep cocktails, and ask the women to wear flapper dresses? I remember a children's book launch where the author dressed as a big yellow bird with stripy legs. These photographs will be around for a long time to come. You and your attendees will post them on social media and share them. How will you like to feel when you see these photos: proud and happy, or slightly awkward?

4. Determine your grand finale

A finale is essential for any book launch. Often, a speech or a reading from the author will suffice. But you can be more inventive than this. One of my clients taped copies of his book beneath the seats of 150 people who attended a property event. They had no idea until he told them to look under their seats. He then asked everyone to look at a certain word on a page inside their books. The person who had the book with the word highlighted in yellow won a £500 prize. The event was fun. Everyone then stood up and gave him a standing ovation. Another author I've worked with enticed people to pay £65 for his book and attend his event, by offering a seminar to teach attendees how to create a successful million-dollar business. How can you surprise or wow your own audience so that you over-deliver on their expectations and they remember your event for a long time to come?

5. Can you attract the media?

Another client of mine wrote an anti-evolution book and invited Ireland's Minister for Science to launch it (though it caused such a controversy that he changed his mind). "Darwin" showed up at the book launch, linking arms with a gorilla. The author had a glass bowl filled with 15 tennis balls which he announced he would dump on the floor to see if they would arrange themselves in a perfect circle. Of course they didn't. The author was delighted when he got media coverage in over 50 newspapers, magazines, radio stations and TV channels.

Another property author I can think of held a book launch at an event near Marble Arch, in London. She held an auction that raised thousands of pounds for a shelter for homeless people, and the event had coverage in various papers including *The Times*.

Why were journalists interested in these events? Because they weren't traditional book launches.

6. Your invitation should excite your attendees

Many authors send out invitations that have an undercurrent of fear and insecurity. You can almost hear the cogs whirring in their head: "What if no one comes?" They say things like: "Please bring along your friends, neighbours and anyone else you know." What can you offer that will make sure they'll move other events in their diary just to be there? Strike a confident tone with your invitation: you're offering a never-to-be-repeated opportunity for a limited number of people. When the tickets are gone, they're gone. They'd be foolish not to come. Offer more than just a book launch and set the tone of your expectations. Take for example, the author who recently held a launch at The Ritz in Mayfair, telling attendees to "dress to impress!" and bring along a business card to share with others.

7. How can you have impact and influence beyond this event?

It's been like sales day at Harrods. People have been desperate for you to sign their books. They've loved your idea. But once the wine or champagne has gone, and guests start to drift away, what longer-term impact will you have? You've had a great event. But what can you do to ensure these people buy your future books, come to other events that you host, or want to work with you? Can you give guests a reason to sign up on your Facebook page, your blog or your newsletter? Can you hand out flyers offering them a free 1-to-1 consultation or taster session? Can you ensure that everyone has your business card or contact details? I've had clients who have trebled their speaking engagements after publishing their book; authors who have generated weekly leads for their business several years after their launch; clients who've got their own magazine columns. What impact will you have?

Pay attention to all these small details and you should have a book launch that really sings!

How Much Should Authors be Paid to Speak at Events?

I was intrigued to read the furore in *The Times* that Joanne Harris, author of *Chocolat*, had pulled out of a book festival because organizers are only paying her a £50 fee. Even more so, that other luminaries such as Philip Pullman were springing to her defence and calling for a boycott of literary festivals that don't pay fees. Of rather more concern to me would have been the fact that festival organizers were trying to tie her into a six-week exclusivity clause – though this was only mentioned as an aside.

As someone who has organized literary festivals and conferences for organizations ranging from the Arts Council of England to Oxford University, as well as being an author-speaker in my own right, I like to think that I can see both sides of the debate.

I know the superhuman effort that goes into organizing an event: working 60-hour weeks and having sleepless nights in order to ensure a full house. I also know what it's like to spend half a day travelling to an event, then be expected to give your all on stage without so much as a loo break or a cup of tea.

First, before we look at the specifics of how much an author should be paid and what can reasonably be expected of you when you speak, let's look at the benefits of speaking at an event and why you might want to do it in the first place:

1. A full house

People mistakenly assume that once an event has been organized, the tickets will automatically sell themselves. This is far from being the case, even if you have an extraordinary line-up of big-name speakers. It can take months of hustle to sell out an event and ensure a full house. This means calling in favours and mailing to other people's newsletters. It means shamelessly asking friends, family, work colleagues, and everyone else you know, to buy tickets. It means promoting the event in newspapers and magazines. It can mean setting up an affiliate scheme so that commission is paid to anyone who sells your tickets. To sum up, it can be a big headache, regardless of whether it's a big event for 1,000 plus or a small event for 50 people. It's a joy to arrive at an event and see that there's standing room only. What you don't see is all the hard work and hassle that brought those people in.

2. Events cost big bucks

A venue for around 500 people in central London can cost around £5,000 to £10,000 per day. That's before you even pay for the extras: the sound system, the speakers, the microphones, the stage, the curtains, the lighting, the roller banners, the flipchart and pens, even the jugs of water at the back of the room. That's before you start offering attendees tea and biscuits or a buffet lunch. Everything in a venue costs money. You're usually expected to book up-front based on numbers that you can't be certain of.

Then, there's the liability insurance and cost of the marketing; the online and offline advertising. All told, the standard costs for hosting a two-day event for 500 people in central London are around £40,000. And the organizer gets to take all the financial risk. Do you really want this level of stress and worry? Are you willing to survive on four hours' sleep per night for weeks on end? Or would you rather keep your sanity and save your energies for writing and promoting your next book?

3. You'll need backup

Every event needs a crew. If there are more than 30 people in the room, you'll need stewards to check tickets and direct people to their seats. You'll need runners to fetch and carry microphones and flipcharts for those speaking. You'll need technicians to put up the staging and lightning, and stick gaffer tape over the wires so that no one trips. You'll need security staff in case there's any trouble. Even if you use volunteers, they'll need refreshments: a breakfast, a lunch or a tea and sometimes all three. When people don't show up due to illness, broken-down cars or injured cats, you'll have the additional worry of how to make do with a team that's several people short.

4. Blowing your own trumpet

Many authors are clueless when it comes to marketing or are wary of sounding like a used car salesman. But as a speaker, someone else blows your trumpet for you. You roll up to a venue amidst fanfare, speak for 90 minutes, then bask in the applause. You sign a few books, have your photo taken with attendees, then you disappear home to a glass of wine.

5. Stress levels

You don't have to worry about clearing up dirty teacups and notepads. You don't have to deal with Mrs Brown who left her favourite scarf under a seat on the back row or her companion who dropped her mobile phone into the toilet in the break. You don't have to worry about the man who punched his neighbour for sitting in his seat or the footlight that set fire to the stage curtain, setting off smoke alarms. You don't have to calm down tipsy speakers who show up several hours late without their

PowerPoint slides; or who swear on stage offending a large percentage of your Muslim audience. Nor do you have to deal with the whinges about the heating at the venue being too hot or too cold, or attendees asking why you're not offering a free organic vegan lunch. (Yes, all these things have happened!) If you choose to speak at an event, rather than hosting one yourself, you are saving yourself from all these distractions.

To sum up: assuming that the festival organizers have done their job properly, you'll be getting massive exposure for little expense or aggro. You get to swan in after all the work has been done, grab the glory, and disappear.

I know dozens of incredibly successful authors all over the world who speak for free. Many of them regularly fly in to London from places like America, Canada or Australia, paying the cost of a long-haul flight and overnight accommodation out of their own pocket.

Why do they do it? Because standing on someone else's stage is a privilege. Because even if they're offered a £10,000 fee, it's a drop in the ocean compared with the amount of clients who sign up with them after an event. Some speakers choose to sell their products (books, DVDs or seminars) at the back of the room and make over six figures in 60 minutes. Others "skim" the room – they simply offer a free gift and invite the participants to sign up to their newsletter or blog. They then contact them at a later date to see if they're interested in their services. Where author-speakers fail to make money from a festival, it's usually because they don't have an enticing or irresistible "call to action". They give their talk, but they don't give their audience a big enough incentive to take action.

So yes, it's great if you're paid as a speaker. But to insist on a fee at all times, and to boycott literary festivals and events that don't pay, in my opinion is short-sighted. When considering an invitation to speak, the main question should not be: "How much am I being paid?" Instead, assess *where* the event is being held, the *type* of people in the audience, the *number* of attendees, and the *track record* of the organizers. The chief question you should ask is: "How much would it cost *me* – timewise and financially – to get this same level of exposure?" Ask for a fee, if you must, but don't make it your be-all and end-all.

Oftentimes you're also rewarded in ways that are more exciting than monetary ones. I gave a couple of marketing talks for members of The Society of Authors for free, a couple of years back. My "reward", though I did not know it at the time, was to be invited to the Queen's Garden Party at Buckingham Palace with my partner. It was a magical day that we'll never forget. Another time, I gave a free talk for post-graduates at Christchurch College, Oxford. I spent that evening dining at high table with the other dons in the historic hall where Harry Potter was filmed. Money simply can't buy these types of experience.

This weekend I'm driving over a hundred miles — a trip of five hours there and back — to speak at a literary festival in Cambridgeshire. I've done this for three years in a row, and I'll be happy to continue for another three. Why? Because I have multiple clients from the previous festivals I spoke at. Because I know what it takes to host an event of that size and calibre. And, because it's a privilege to be there.

What I Learned From Selling Books From the Back of My Car

We were standing shivering, looking at a big stack of books in the boot of my car. It was a cold and cloudy day at a car boot sale in a field in Oxfordshire. Most people who wandered past us looked grumpy. Moreover, there was some sort of sorcery in the air: my daughters and I seemed to be suddenly invisible. For as people approached our car, they either looked right through us or looked away.

We took a foldaway table out of the car and tried to arrange the books attractively on it. But after 30 minutes, we had sold a big fat ZERO.

My daughters, Chiara (aged eight) and Tierni (aged nine) had started out enthusiastically, but were beginning to look a bit crestfallen: "No one wants to buy them, Mummy. We should go home," they whispered. "This is embarrassing. *Really* embarrassing!"

They'd written and illustrated their books for fun in their holidays and had asked me if I would publish them. "I want to be an author like you, Mummy," Tierni had said. "Me too," echoed Chiara. "Why not?" I'd thought. I help adults to write and publish books every day, but it'd never occurred to me to help my own children do the same thing. They'd both been having problems with bullying at school, so it seemed like a good idea to boost their self-esteem. I had optimistically booked a pitch at a local car boot sale shortly after the books were published, thinking that it would help rebuild the girls' confidence to sell some of their books there.

Except now we were at the front line, as it were. It was time to sell the darned things ... and reality was proving a little different to my expectations.

I wondered, momentarily, if my kids had more of a handle on this than I did. Maybe it was a mistake after all. Maybe we should pack up our stack of books and go home.

Then, I looked at their disappointed little faces.

If you're a parent, you'll know that feeling of your child's pain being your pain. You'll also know there's no bigger incentive to spur you on to accomplish things you'd never normally consider.

There was no way I was going to admit defeat and drive home. We had to turn this around somehow or other. So instead of standing quietly behind our table of books, passively waiting for sales to just *happen*, I started to take a more proactive approach. You've most likely seen those traders hawking strawberries and raspberries from their market stalls? Well, I decided to take a leaf out of their book and start calling out to passers-by.

This seemed to be an instant antidote to our invisibility. People started looking at us curiously, even if it was just because they were thinking: "Who is that insanely loud woman and what the bloody hell does she want?"

A lady, with an Australian accent, was the first to come over to our stall. We watched with baited breath while she started leafing through Tierni's book, *The Queen of the Dogs*.

"You did all this yourself? Without any help?" she asked, shaking her head in disbelief.

My daughter beamed broadly. "I did," she nodded.

"Then, I'd better get your autograph in case you get famous later on," the woman said, hooking out her purse.

She handed over a banknote and Tierni gave her the change; a big smile on her face. The tip of her tongue poked out on her lip as she wrote her name with a flourish: her first ever autograph.

It was our first customer. But she'd also given us a couple of powerful ideas to try out. Instead of thinking about *selling* books, we started to invite people to take a look inside them at the illustrations. We weren't expecting money or even sales. We were inviting people to be inspired and entertained.

Once there was no pressure or expectation to buy, people started coming and looking in droves. And the more people surrounded our car, the more that other people followed them out of curiosity!

We chatted about incidental things: where they were from; what they'd bought at other stalls; their families. Then, effortlessly, without encouragement, they bought the books for their own children and grandchildren. They bought the books not just because they liked the illustrations or the stories, but because they also felt inspired and uplifted. "It might encourage our kids to write books too," they said. It was their emotional experience of the books, and the relevance to their own lives, that hooked them in.

Often, the adults were torn between *The Cat with No Name* (Chiara's book) and *The Queen of the Dogs* (Tierni's book). There was a bit of a competition going on between my daughters to see which book would sell more: the "cat" book or the "dog" book. Seeing a potential quarrel looming, this helped me to get creative. So we started offering a "special deal": a two-book bundle at a discounted price. After this, the girls' books really started flying off the table.

An hour or so later, we'd sold over 100 books and the girls had signed most of them. They were tired, but happy, and wandered off to spend some of their hard-earned coins on Mr Whippy ice creams with milk chocolate flakes.

When they came back, there was another treat in store. A local businessman who was passing was so impressed with their initiative, that he'd given them a donation to write their next books. "I used to wash my dad's car for *my* pocket money," he said.

"That was in the old days," Chiara grinned cheekily. "We're authors: we sell books!"

The Author

Stephanie J. Hale is a writing coach and publishing expert who has worked with fiction and non-fiction authors for over 20 years – helping them to write, sell and promote their books.

She is author of award-winning books including: Millionaire Author, How to Sell One Million Books and Millionaire Property Author.

She is former Assistant Director of the world-famous creative writing course at Oxford University. She founded Oxford Literary Consultancy in 2004.

She was awarded a British Empire Medal for services to authors by Her Majesty the Queen in 2017.

The Authors' Vault
FREE Training and Bonuses
Specially for You

- Topics include:
- How to Find a Publisher or Literary Agent.
- How to Choose a Bestselling Book Title.
- Mistakes to Avoid with Agents and Publishers.
- Red Flags to Look Out For in a Publishing Contract.
- How to Write a Marketing Plan for Your Book.
- Can I Quote Someone Without Permission?
- Should I Use 50 Shades of X as a Book Title?
- How to Write Your Book Faster.
- How to Choose the Best Book Cover.
- Should I Self-Publish or is a Mainstream Publisher Better?
- How to Sell More Copies of your Book.
- How to Stop Other Authors Stealing Your Book Idea.
- Should I Disguise Real-Life Characters?
- How to Get Celebrity Endorsements.
- And much more ...

Register for your free reports at:

www.CelebrityAuthorsSecrets.com/vault

Oxford Literary Consultancy
Publishing Services

- Manuscript evaluation – confidential feedback of your book's marketability.

- Proofreading and editing – with fast-track service.

- Book cover design and typesetting.

- PR campaigns – publicity in magazines, newspapers, radio and TV.

- Ghostwriting.

- Mentoring.

Our consultants work for publishers including: Bloomsbury, HarperCollins, Hodder & Stoughton, Little Brown, Simon & Schuster and Random House.

Find out whether your book idea is marketable.

Book a free 20-minute consultation today!

www.oxfordwriters.com

www.ingramcontent.com/pod-product-compliance
Ingram Content Group UK Ltd.
Pitfield, Milton Keynes, MK11 3LW, UK
UKHW042004230426
12048UKWH00009B/546